DOROTHY PORTER WESLEY
at
HOWARD UNIVERSITY

DOROTHY PORTER WESLEY
at
HOWARD UNIVERSITY
Building a Legacy of Black History

JANET SIMS-WOOD, PHD
with the assistance of Charlynn Spencer Pyne

Foreword by Dr. Thomas C. Battle | *Afterword by Mr. Howard Dodson*

Charleston   London

THE
History
PRESS

Published by The History Press
Charleston, SC 29403
www.historypress.net

Copyright © 2014 by Janet Sims-Wood
All rights reserved

First published 2014

ISBN 978-1-5402-1120-0

Library of Congress CIP data applied for.

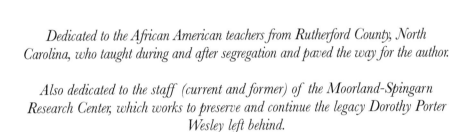

Dedicated to the African American teachers from Rutherford County, North Carolina, who taught during and after segregation and paved the way for the author.

Also dedicated to the staff (current and former) of the Moorland-Spingarn Research Center, which works to preserve and continue the legacy Dorothy Porter Wesley left behind.

CONTENTS

CONTENTS

Contents

FOREWORD

We value books and libraries, but we often overlook the custodians who collect and care for them so that the resources are available to us whenever we need them. We enjoy historical artifacts and documents that illuminate our past, but we often overlook those who preserve them. We marvel at the images captured in the various media we have developed, but we often ignore those who seek them out and save them for our enlightenment. We value the work of scholars who use the resources, but we tend to ignore the keepers and bibliophiles who make the scholarship possible. Many of these keepers (librarians, curators, archivists) had a wide-ranging knowledge of a myriad of subjects, which assisted researchers in probing more deeply into little-known and unknown areas of scholarship. Some of these keepers became scholars unto themselves. One was Dorothy Porter Wesley, a legend to scholars of black history and culture.

Dorothy Porter Wesley was part of a generation that helped to foster a new understanding of the black experience in Africa, the Americas and other parts of the world. Since much of the history of people of African descent was intentionally fabricated, ignored or obscured in efforts to justify enslavement, cultural ostracism and institutional racism, that history and materials documenting that history were essentially deemed of little or no importance. Efforts to correct this were hampered by indifference, intentional obfuscation, ignorance and a lack of oral, documentary and material evidence to substantiate claims that contradicted the notion that black people had no meaningful history and had made no significant contributions.

On the occasion of Porter Wesley's retirement from Howard University, historian Benjamin Quarles noted the former's contributions to Africana scholarship by opining that there was no significant work in black history in the post–World War II era that did not acknowledge and benefit from her efforts. Those efforts extended beyond the collection of books, periodicals and published scholarship. Porter Wesley ferreted out and valued obscure items that scholars would later realize were valuable. These scraps of paper, letters, diaries, journals, scrapbooks, photographs and ephemeral items became the jewels of research. In addition to the wise counsel she offered, which reflected her own scholarship, Porter Wesley developed bibliographies and special library cataloguing that would better enable students and scholars of black history to access important information. Her accomplishments are reflected in the many awards she received from the various professional and scholarly communities that benefitted from her decades-long efforts.

Upon Porter Wesley's retirement in 1973, Howard University reorganized the collections she had overseen for more than forty years as the Moorland-Spingarn Research Center (MSRC). As the MSRC celebrates its centennial, it is only fitting that we reexamine a life of service that seems more a calling than a career. It is also fitting that Dr. Janet Sims-Wood authored this biography. She was inspired by Porter Wesley and mirrors her as she continues in the tradition of scholar/librarian.

THOMAS C. BATTLE, PHD
Retired Director
Moorland-Spingarn Research Center
Howard University

Acknowledgements

So many people contributed to the completion of this book. Thanks to Prince George's Community College (PGCC) for the Pathfinder Grant that allowed me to travel to Yale University to conduct research in the Dorothy Porter Wesley Papers. Also, all of my co-workers in the PGCC library were very helpful and supportive, especially during the last weeks, when they graciously changed schedules to accommodate my time away from the library.

Ida Jones is responsible for introducing me to The History Press. I appreciate her support as I prepared my proposal and in guiding me to materials in the Moorland-Spingarn Research Center.

I spent a week at the Beinecke Rare Book and Manuscript Library at Yale University conducting research in the Dorothy Porter Wesley Papers. I was only able to go through eighteen of the more than one hundred boxes of materials, but the staff was most helpful in getting me reproductions and photographs from this collection. Research librarian Karen Nangle was my contact person and worked to help me get research materials. I am truly grateful to all of the staff (librarians, technicians and security) for their assistance. Thanks to Yale student Julie Botnick for her insights on Porter.

My "adopted son," Yohuru Williams, associate vice-president for academic affairs at Fairfield University, gave me the opportunity to speak to the students during my trip to Connecticut.

Thanks to Thomas C. Battle, retired director of the Moorland-Spingarn Research Center, who worked with Dorothy Porter during her last years at

Howard University. He not only wrote the foreword but also gave personal perceptions on working with Porter.

The staff of the Moorland-Spingarn Research Center went above and beyond the call of research assistance in helping me find information. Thanks to JoEllen ElBashir, Ida Jones, Kenvi Phillips and Richard Jenkins in the Manuscript Division; Clifford Muse, Tewodros "Teddy" Abebe and Lopez Matthews in the Archives; and Ishmael Childs and Amber Junipher in the Reference Department. All of you were most helpful, and I owe you a debt of gratitude for your unending support and for long-standing friendships. Current Moorland-Spingarn director Howard Dodson also provided the afterword.

Darlene Clark Hine, John Bracey, Sharon Harley, Randall Burkett, Ruby Sales, Dolores Leffall, Yvonne Seon, Elinor Des Verney Sinnette and Marilyn Richardson were so gracious in relating their personal experiences with Dorothy Porter. Their comments showed Porter as a real person.

W. Paul Coates, founder of Black Classic Press, gave special insight into the black bibliophiles whom Porter loved and on the Black Bibliophiles and Collectors symposium held at Howard University. He published two works by Porter—a reprint of her *Early Negro Writing, 1760–1837* and *William Cooper Nell, Nineteenth-Century African American Abolitionist, Historian, Integrationist: Selected Writings, 1832–1874*, which was completed by Porter's daughter, Constance Porter Uzelac.

Kenya King, journalist and actress, helped me find information on the White House photo Porter took with President Bill Clinton at the National Endowment for the Humanities Charles Frankel Prize celebration.

Thanks to Karen Bowlding, who served as a guide to get the project off the ground with valuable research and editorial assistance.

I give thanks to my family for always supporting me in whatever project I undertake. My friends from high school, college, work and church always gave me encouragement to continue on, even when I was tired. I thank them all for their prayers.

Last but not least, I need to give special thanks to Charlynn Spencer Pyne, who came on to help copyedit this book. Charlynn took on so much more than copyediting, and her support has been invaluable. As a Howard University graduate (history) and a former reference librarian at the Moorland-Spingarn Research Center, Charlynn brought historical knowledge and expertise to the project that was pertinent in helping the reader see Dorothy Porter Wesley as a vital part of Washington, D.C., and Howard University history.

PREFACE

As we commemorate the 100th anniversary of Howard University's Moorland-Spingarn Research Center, a biography of Dorothy Porter Wesley is in order. This is not only a biography but also a tribute that captures the memories of people who came in contact with Porter at various times and events in her life.

Because she had two husbands—James A. Porter and Charles H. Wesley—she is sometimes called Porter and sometimes Wesley. She and Wesley married late in life, so she will be called Porter throughout the text of this book.

Porter earned bachelor of science (BS) and master of science (MS) degrees in library science from the Columbia University School of Library Service in 1931 and 1932, respectively, and was the first African American woman to do so. The dates cited above are the ones given by Porter in her curriculum vitae (dated 1972) and in several interviews. However, according to Yale University student Julie Botnick, there is a discrepancy regarding the dates that Porter graduated from Columbia. Botnick writes, "There has been a perpetuated historical inaccuracy regarding the year she received her MLS [*sic*]. Every modern secondary source lists her as completing her bachelor's degree in 1931 and her master's degree in 1932. However, the program from her Columbia graduation ceremony shows she received her master's on June 2, 1931."

And while most of Porter's contemporaries have passed on, there is a cadre of people who were students, researchers and scholars whom she helped during and after her tenure at Howard University.

This is not the definitive biography on Porter, as that still needs to be written. Her collection was auctioned to Yale University by the Swann Auction Galleries via the William Reese Company in March 2012, with additional material coming in July and November 2012 after the death of her daughter, Constance Porter Uzelac. It is open to the pubic but as an unprocessed collection. Since the collection is unprocessed, it was difficult to go through. Materials seemed to be thrown in boxes, and although the boxes sometimes said materials inside dealt with a certain time period or subject, there were similar items in other boxes as well. That made it very hard to really get a sense of Porter's life and accomplishments. There was even dental floss in one of the boxes.

Thus, I was only able to go through 18 of the 137 boxes of materials on her in the Yale University collection. I missed a lot of pertinent information by not being able to look at all the boxes in the collection.

The definitive biography should be written after the collection at Yale is processed along with the James Amos Porter Papers at Emory University and the Charles Harris Wesley papers housed with the Alpha Phi Alpha fraternity. All three collections, as well as other collections with materials on Porter, are vital to understanding the magnitude of her contributions.

One of the highlights of my Yale research trip was meeting Julie Botnick, a senior at Yale who was writing a paper on Porter. When Botnick asked for certain boxes, she was told that I had already checked them out. So she approached me, introduced herself and agreed to a short interview. She stated that her interest in libraries and archives was the motivating factor for her work on Porter. She planned to focus her paper on the time when Porter was a student at Columbia University, how her interest in library science shaped her life, Porter's career at Howard University and her trip to Europe with James Porter in 1935.

I asked Botnick what she thought of Porter as a person. She said, "I like her. There are so many events where she could have strayed from her path, but she stayed the course." It was wonderful indeed to see a young person with an interest in the life's work of a woman who was so instrumental in helping to develop libraries and archives throughout the world. Botnick's paper can be found on the Yale University website.

This book is a tribute to a woman on whose shoulders I still stand. Although she was retired from the Moorland-Spingarn Research Center before I came on board as a reference librarian and African American history specialist, I had the privilege of talking with Porter during her visits to the center, and I often visited her home.

On one occasion, I visited Porter's home with Jean Blackwell Hutson, who served as a curator and then as chief of the Schomburg Center for Research in Black Culture. Widely known for her cooking skills, Porter prepared a delicious meal for us. Sitting with two icons who headed large libraries documenting Africana materials was truly a treat. There were lots of memories shared and laughter enjoyed by those two women that day.

Porter's support of others was invaluable, and some have spoken of her help in this volume. She was especially helpful to those doing research in women's studies. I sought out Porter's counsel when I began writing and publishing my own bibliographies on African Americans. She would often review my work and offer suggestions. Porter's wisdom and tidbits of advice will always be remembered and cherished.

Esme Bhan, in an article titled "Dorothy Louise Burnett Porter" and published in *Washington History* (Spring–Summer 1996), noted that "Bag Lady" was the moniker given to Porter for going into basements and attics looking for material. "Librarian-scholar" was the nickname given to her by Howard University professor Arthur P. Davis for her research skills and publishing. "Librarian Extraordinaire" was what Librarian of Congress James H. Billington called her for "her vital role in setting precepts for bibliophiles in the art of collecting African-Americana."

Dorothy Porter Wesley at Howard University: Building a Legacy of Black History is composed of seven chapters. Chapter 1, "Dorothy Burnett Porter Wesley: The Early Years, 1905–25," details her life from birth up through 1925, when she graduated from Miner Normal School. Chapter 2, "Howard University: The Early Years, 1867–1926," describes the founding of Howard University up to Porter's enrollment as a student and work as a student assistant in the library. Chapter 3, "Collecting and Organizing Africana Materials at Howard University," examines Porter as she came on full time in the library at Howard and continued her pursuit of a library degree. This chapter addresses the hard work and perseverance that went into building the Africana collections, planning for the Howard University Museum and acquiring the Arthur B. Spingarn Collection and other notable acquisitions. Chapter 4, "A Meeting Place for Researchers at Howard University," explores her relationship with the many researchers, scholars, collectors and bibliophiles who came to the library for assistance. Chapter 5, "Documenting the Africana Experience," looks at her research that added to the body of work in the field and also examines her work with organizations and institutions such as the African Studies

Association, the American Antiquarian Society, the Association for the Study of African American Life and History and others. Chapter 6, "Librarian/Curator Emerita," details her activities after her official retirement from Howard University. Chapter 7, "The Dorothy Porter Wesley Collections," examines the Dorothy Porter Wesley Collection at the Broward County Library in Fort Lauderdale, Florida, and the massive Dorothy Porter Wesley Papers in the Beinecke Rare Book and Manuscript Library at Yale University. There are also two appendices: "Awards and Accolades Received by Dorothy Porter Wesley" and "A Selected Bibliography of Publications by Dorothy Porter Wesley."

The Negro Collection, the Moorland Collection and the Moorland Foundation: A Library of Negro Life are used synonymously, but Porter preferred the name Moorland Foundation. In addition, Porter and other researchers often referred to the collection as the Moorland Room. In "Dorothy Porter Wesley: A Bio-Bibliographic Profile," published in *American Women in the Arts and Social Sciences: A Bibliographic Survey*, Helen Britton writes that the name was changed to the Moorland-Spingarn Collection in 1958. In 1973, the Moorland-Spingarn Collection was reorganized as a separate administrative unit, and the Moorland-Spingarn Research Center was created. In this book, I call the collection the Moorland Foundation from 1930 to mid-1973, except in direct quotes. From June 1973 onward, I refer to the collection as the Moorland-Spingarn Research Center or MSRC.

This book is just a glimpse into the importance of Porter, a librarian par excellence who influenced the scholarly community not only in Washington, D.C, but throughout the world by collecting, organizing and preserving material by and about persons of African descent. Her life's mission lives on in the librarians and archivists who continue to follow in her footsteps.

Chapter 1

DOROTHY BURNETT PORTER WESLEY: THE EARLY YEARS, 1905–25

EARLY LIFE

Dorothy Burnett Porter Wesley, daughter of physician Hayes Joseph Burnett Sr. and Bertha Ball Burnett, was born on May 25, 1905, in Warrenton, Virginia. She grew up in Montclair, New Jersey, in a middle-class Irish Catholic neighborhood. Not much is written about her parents and childhood, but two research papers—one written in 1972 and the other in 2014—reveal more of her early life. The 1972 paper, titled "A Brief Study of Mrs. Dorothy Burnett Porter: From Birth to Completion of High School, 1905–1922," was written by Janice M. Muganda for Rayford Logan's "Negro in the Modern World" class at Howard University. It details Porter's childhood from recorded and unrecorded interviews conducted by Muganda on December 18 and 19, 1971, at Porter's home in Washington, D.C. Muganda also interviewed Porter's sister, Leonie B. Harper, on January 6, 1972. The second paper, "'I Am Sure That You Know Yourself That It Is a Very Good Job': The Early Life and Library of Dorothy Porter," was written by Julie Botnick for John Gaddis's 2014 "The Art of Biography" class at Yale University. Botnick's research is based on material found in Porter's papers at Yale University. The Muganda paper is part of the Dorothy Porter Wesley Papers, housed in the Yale University Beinecke Rare Book & Manuscript Library. Botnick's paper can be found on the Yale University website. Much of the information about Porter's parents and childhood is taken from these unpublished papers.

Porter was the eldest of four children. Her siblings were Hayes Joseph Jr., Leonie and Alice. Her father, born in 1877, was a 1904 graduate of the Howard University School of Medicine and was the first African American doctor to practice medicine in Montclair. He was also a founding member of the Montclair National Association for the Advancement of Colored People (NAACP). In a letter Gustee Burnett, Hayes Sr.'s brother, wrote to Porter on January 30, 1936, he noted that Hayes had several full and half brothers and sisters but that he did not have pictures of the family. Hayes was not involved with his family even though Gustee tried to communicate with him.

Porter's mother was born as Roberta Ball in 1887 in Virginia. She was sent to Boston to get the education she could not get in Virginia. According to her unpublished memoir, a teacher changed her name to Bertha in the school records, and she was known as Bertha for the rest of her life. Although she was thought to be behind because she came from the South, Bertha worked hard and was promoted several grades in school. Bertha met Hayes Burnett in New York City. They were married within three months, with their first child arriving soon after. Bertha was a homemaker and tennis player who helped organize the New Jersey Tennis Association. In her memoir, Bertha further states that the marriage was cold and that she and her husband eventually stopped communicating with each other.

Because her father purchased books instead of frivolous items, Porter developed a love for reading. He had her read the dictionary. Whenever she did not know the meaning of a word, he would tell her to look it up and then had her explain what each word in the definition meant. Among the many books in his library were books on literature and history. There were also dictionaries, encyclopedias and medical books—including histories of medicine.

Porter did not study black history while growing up. She could not remember there being a lot of books by and about blacks in her home, as not many books by black authors were published during that time. In her essay titled "Fifty Years of Collecting," published in Richard Newman's 1984 book *Black Access: A Bibliography of Afro-American Bibliographies*, Porter remembered:

> *The poetry of Paul Laurence Dunbar was among the books on the bookshelf. His poetry was very familiar as my mother frequently recited his poetry at the Methodist church we attended...Kelly Miller, a famous sociologist whom my father had known while he was a student at Howard University, was on occasion a guest in our home where some of his books and pamphlets were to be found. I also remember being raised up onto my*

father's shoulders to see Booker T. Washington on one of his speaking tours in the area...I believe most black families such as ours possessed his Up from Slavery. *My personal copy of* Iola Leroy, *the first novel by a black woman, Frances Ellen Watkins Harper, was among my father's library.*

The family was well cared for, living in a large corner home at 33 Maple Place with a garden and a garage in the back. In describing her home life to Muganda, Porter noted, "I think that growing up in an atmosphere of beauty, not only interior of a building, but the outside where there were gardens, trees and flowers had an influence on me throughout my life." Muganda also learned that Porter enjoyed horse-and-buggy rides with her father as he made house calls. His first mode of transportation had been a bicycle until a well-known Montclair physician, James Spencer Brown, gave him the horse and buggy. A caring and dedicated physician, Burnett often stayed up nights with maternity cases and returned fees to those who could not afford to pay him.

Porter's father was active in community affairs and ran for coroner in 1914 and for commissioner in 1916. Muganda located an article about his candidacy in the June 24, 1916 *Montclair Times* that asserted:

> *His candidacy marks a new epoch in the political life of the Colored citizens of Montclair, bringing them into the limelight of public affairs, where their race loyalty, civic pride, and self-confidence are to be weighed to the balance of public opinion...We must have men who have self-confidence, courage of convictions, and [be thoroughly] democratic. With Dr. Burnett leading the way, the Colored voters of Montclair have an opportunity of a life-time to evidence their ability and to solidify and fight for the recognition long withheld.*

Porter's mother taught Sunday school at St. Mark's Methodist Church in Montclair and probably inspired Porter to teach Sunday school as well. As a tennis player, the mother helped organize the Oriole Tennis Club and often played women's doubles with Lucy Diggs Slowe, the former dean of women at Howard University. Ranking third in the Negro Women National Championships, Bertha also taught Porter how to play tennis.

Neither parent was a strong disciplinarian. Porter admitted to Muganda that "my father thought my mother should discipline us, and my mother thought my father should discipline us. Sometimes my mother would punish me by sending me to bed. This did not bother me because I always hid books and a bottle of olives under my mattress."

During the summer months, Porter and her friends would sell lemonade for five cents a glass. She also attended sewing bees one Saturday a month. In the sewing class, she made aprons and skirts and did fancy embroidering and crocheting. Porter recalled making a dress copied from a display in the window of a New York shop on Fifth Avenue. The skirt of that dress was covered with tiny chiffon roses that had to be made one by one.

Porter's brother, Hayes Jr., called her "Queenie" because she enjoyed home life—helping with the cleaning, cooking and sewing for the family. In Muganda's January 6, 1972 interview with Porter's sister, Leonie B. Harper, she observed that, "She [Dorothy] was a strange child. She couldn't keep still, always reading, sewing, teaching piano or cooking. She didn't believe in Santa Claus like other children her age."

A fond memory that Porter related to Muganda was of the Campfire Girls. She recalled, "Something about the ritual appealed to me—the candlelight, the beaded work, the leather dresses that we wore and the various stages in the Campfire life."

She also told Muganda that the hobbies she enjoyed were swimming, roller-skating and tennis. And Porter's favorite hobby was ice-skating. She fondly remembered, "When it was very cold, school was dismissed, and we would always look from a window at home towards the Town Hall, where a white flag with a red circle in the center was flown. That meant the pond or lake was frozen and skating would be permitted that day…This was a great holiday. We would skate all day, enjoying hot chocolate and sandwiches which were sold in a house near the lake."

Porter also loved flowers, roses in particular. She told Muganda that her interest was stimulated and encouraged by her next-door neighbor Mr. Brooks, who taught her how to graft roses, thus enabling each of them to have several varieties in their gardens. She recalled, "We often worked together in each other's yards. I had so many varieties of roses one year that I wrote an operetta which I entitled 'Quarrel Among the Flowers.' Each rose was competing with the other to determine who would become the queen because of beauty, color and fragrance."

EDUCATION

Porter attended a private kindergarten before going to Spaulding Elementary School and entered Hillside Junior High School in the seventh grade. As a child, she enjoyed studying nature and languages, including Latin and Spanish. Nature studies included hikes through the woods, where the students identified plants, trees, wildflowers and birds. Sometimes the students brought their lunch, as the walks would often last an entire afternoon.

Porter remembered her friends as being very studious, noting that they often visited one another's homes to study Latin and drink hot chocolate. Picnics and visits to museums and libraries were an integral part of her educational activities.

Porter started piano lessons at age seven, learning from two private teachers. During her last years in high school, she taught piano lessons to very young children who lived in the neighboring towns of Glenridge and Bloomfield, New Jersey. She earned one dollar per lesson, which she used to supplement her allowance. While at Hillside, she played piano for the school orchestra, the only girl and the only black in the orchestra. As a pianist, Porter accompanied several singers and violinists who would give concerts at the St. Mark's Episcopal Church in East Orange, New Jersey, the church where she was christened. One of the church concerts in which she played was given to interest people in the Marcus Garvey movement. Porter told Muganda:

> *Sousa's Marches were not easy to play because the fingers of my left hand were small and weak and the conductor of the orchestra was always directing me to "play the left hand a little louder." At any rate I lived through many rehearsals where I very proudly played the piano as the only girl and the only Negro student in the orchestra. I can still see the conductor pointing his baton at me.*

Porter was not very impressed with her high school, as some of her teachers were prejudiced. Her parents and the principal had frequent discussions. According to Muganda, one such topic of discussion occurred when her section teacher insisted that Porter take commercial art courses instead of college prep courses. Porter observed:

> *My teachers were not too kind to me. My French teacher told me that I would never be able to speak French well because my lips were too thick, and I spent many days trying to stretch them thinking this would thin them. I was given a part in Shakespeare's* The Tempest, *and I also remember appearing in a dance in our beautiful amphitheater.*

During her high school years, Porter was a member of the Blue Birds, a social club that was made up of girls from different suburban neighborhoods. According to Muganda, Porter was also a member of the Young Women's Christian Association:

> *I was a very ardent worker of the Montclair Y.W.C.A. I remember many evenings going there for activities and the lovely walk I had home from the Y.W.C.A. which was probably ten or fifteen blocks from my home. It always was a rush to get home before the town clock struck 9:00 p.m. We had to be home by 9:00. Very often we had deep snows, and it was very enjoyable walking through the crisp white snow in the evenings on the way home.*

Porter was one of 6 black students of the 250 graduating seniors at Montclair High School. During that same year, tragedy struck. She sadly noted to Muganda that her father became ill and diagnosed himself with pulmonary tuberculosis. He went into a sanitarium, telling his family that he would be gone before Thanksgiving. He passed that November.

Julie Botnick noted in her research paper that, as a widow, Bertha was financially and emotionally challenged. Her second marriage to James Sadler was a drain on her already fragile existence. Sadler died in 1946.

After high school, Porter moved in 1923 to Washington, D.C., to attend Miner Normal School. This was her first experience in the segregated South. Growing up in a largely white community, she was shielded from some of the racism that existed during that time, although she did experience discrimination by some of her teachers. One of the first acts of discrimination she experienced in Washington, D.C., was that blacks could not sit and read in the District of Columbia Public Library. This was difficult for Porter, who had always enjoyed going to her local public library and especially the children's room.

Porter attended Miner Normal School on the recommendation of Julia E. Brooks, a Washington, D.C. high school assistant principal and dean of Women at Dunbar High School. Brooks, a friend of Porter's mother, encouraged the young girl to become a teacher. Her parents were strong advocates of education and encouraged their children to gain as much knowledge as possible.

Public higher education for the District of Columbia originated in 1851, when Myrtilla Miner founded a school for "colored girls." Miner had been denied permission to teach African American girls while working at the Newton Female Institute in Whitesville, Mississippi. In 1879, Miner Normal School joined the District of Columbia Public School System. In 1929, it became Miner Teacher's College, merging in 1955 with Wilson Teacher's College (for white students) to form the District of Columbia Teacher's College, which then became part of the University of the District of Columbia in 1976.

At Miner Normal School, Porter's passion for books led to her calling as a librarian. While there, she was mentored by librarian Lula V. Allan. The two became good friends, as both had an avid interest in books. Allan was a graduate of Simmons College Library School and served as a librarian at Howard University from 1909 to 1920. During Porter's last year at Miner Normal School, Allan became ill, and Porter was asked to manage the library, with the approval of Miner Normal School principal, Eugene Clark.

On June 17, 1925, Porter received her teaching diploma from Miner Normal School and, according to her essay in *Black Access*, started the summer session in library science at Columbia University. In a footnote in her paper, Botnick notes the discrepancy in the dates when Porter attended Columbia University. She writes, "…in her Rosenwald fund application she lists the summer of 1927, 1928, 1929, and 1931 as semesters of coursework toward her bachelor's and lists 1930–1931 as years dedicated to her master's." In addition, Melvil Dewey, who opened the nation's first library science school at Columbia College (now Columbia University) in 1887, moved the school two years later to Albany, New York, where it became the New York State Library School. It did not return to Columbia until 1926.

During those summer sessions at Columbia's Library School, Porter commuted from her home in Montclair, as she was not allowed to stay in the dormitory. In her essay in *Black Access*, Porter detailed the long commute:

I commuted from my home in Montclair to Columbia University by way of Hoboken, arriving at Columbia University in the morning for all-day courses and leaving the Countee Cullen Library in Harlem at 9:00 p.m. when it closed, for the trip back to New Jersey. I did not really mind this, in spite of the fact that the subway trains were often crowded. I sometimes read with a book in my left hand while standing and holding on to the overhead strap with my right hand, during the long ride from 135th Street to South Ferry, where I took the Lackawanna train to New Jersey. By the time the train arrived at the Montclair depot the stars were usually out.

While attending classes, Porter also worked part-time evenings at the 135th Street Branch Library's circulation desk and in the Division of Negro

Literature, History and Prints (later the Schomburg Center for Research in Black Culture). She had a good example of what a librarian should be in branch librarian Ernestine Rose.

In writing about Ernestine Rose in the summer 2011 issue of *Long Island History Journal*, Ann Sanford notes that Rose, a white woman, became the first librarian in a major city to assemble an integrated professional staff. Rose felt that the most important duty of the library was to lead intellectual thought through book clubs, publishing book reviews and with story hours for children. She sponsored activities at the library such as evening book discussions and lectures that were open to all, as well as art events to stimulate race consciousness.

Porter continued working and attending classes at Columbia. In her article in *Black Access*, she noted that she had a keen interest in books and remembered a significant and interesting literary event in her life that occurred in 1925:

> *As a reader of* Survey Graphic *magazine, I was excited about the March 1925 special issue,* Harlem, Mecca of the New Negro, *edited by Alain Leroy Locke* [and devoted to the Harlem Renaissance]. *I still have in my own library two copies which I bought fifty-one years ago for fifty cents a copy...Among several articles it contained "Enter the New Negro," by Alain Leroy Locke...Locke* [also] *prepared for the* Survey Graphic *a well-rounded bibliography, "The Negro in Print: A Selected List of Magazines and Books By and About the Negro."*

So, with credits from both Miner Normal School and Columbia University, Porter enrolled as a full-time student at Howard University to obtain an AB degree. She would also continue her studies during the summers at Columbia in pursuit of her library science degrees.

Chapter 2

HOWARD UNIVERSITY:
THE EARLY YEARS, 1867–1926

*Be it enacted by the Senate and the House of Representatives of the United States
of America, in Congress Assembled, That there be established, and is hereby
established, in the District of Columbia, a university for the education of youth
in the liberal arts and sciences, under the name, style and title of "The Howard
University." Approved March 2, 1867, 14 United States Statutes at Large, 438*
—*Rayford Logan,* Howard University: The First Hundred Years,
1867–1967 *(1968)*

The year 1926, the year in which Porter enrolled in Howard University,
was a pivotal one in the history of the university. That year, Mordecai
W. Johnson became the university's first African American president. Over
the next thirty-four years, he would lead, transform and grow the university
into the largest and most renowned black university in the world by 1960,
when his tenure came to a close.

THE FOUNDING

Howard University was the brainchild of the First Congregational Society
of Washington, D.C. (which later became the First Congregational Church
and is now the First Congregational United Church of Christ), located at 945
G Street NW. The church's first minister, C.B. Boynton, who concurrently

served as chaplain of the U.S. House of Representatives, proposed in November 1866 that it establish a theological seminary to educate African American clergymen.

By the time the charter was issued four months later on March 2, 1867, the idea of a seminary had blossomed to that of a university. Section five of the charter organized the departments of normal (i.e., teacher education), college prep, theology, law, medicine and agriculture, as well as "such others as the board of trustees may establish." The Normal Department opened two months later, followed by the Preparatory Department, which was designed to prepare students for college-level work. Soon to follow were the Theology Department, the Law Department and the Medical Department. The remaining department delineated in the charter, an agricultural department, "was never organized with a curriculum that would justify the name," writes Logan in *Howard University: The First Hundred Years, 1867–1967*.

Howard University was named for Oliver Otis Howard, a general in the army, an active member of First Congregational Church and one of the seventeen university founders to whom the charter was issued. He was also a Civil War hero and the first commissioner of the Bureau of Refugees, Freedmen and Abandoned Lands, popularly known as the Freedmen's Bureau. The Freedmen's Bureau was established by President Abraham Lincoln in March 1865 to assist persons who were formerly enslaved. However, it lost most of its funding in 1869 and was disbanded by President Ulysses S. Grant in June 1872.

Howard, while remaining on active duty in the army and serving as the commissioner of the Freedmen's Bureau, also took on the presidency of the university, serving in that capacity from April 1869 to November 1873.

From the university's beginning, the Freedmen's Bureau under Howard provided most of the financial support, as it did for approximately twenty-five other African American colleges. And in 1879, six years after the Freedmen's Bureau's demise, the federal government began annual appropriations to Howard University that continue to the present day as one of the university's major sources of funds.

When Howard University opened on May 1, 1867, the first students were young white women—the daughters of members of the board of trustees and also members of First Congregational Church. And while, over the years, some would point to this fact as proof that the university was founded to "educate youth" regardless of sex and race, the early decades were a period of transition during which the university would remain cosmopolitan while becoming predominantly black.

In *Howard University: The Capstone of Negro Education, A History: 1867–1940* (1941), Walter Dyson states that in 1904, university president John Gordon,

> *observing that the University was "drawing young men from Cuba, Porto [sic] Rico, Barbados, Trinidad, Japan…and from South America, and Asia and Africa," declared in his inaugural address that "the directing hand of God" was assisting in making Howard University a school for the "colored races of all the continents"…"and I am sure," he continued, "that we shall find notable educators who will dedicate themselves, and men and women who will dedicate their estates to the work of making Howard the University of all the colored races."*

THE CAMPUS

The first classes were held in a former German dance hall and beer saloon located on Georgia Avenue below W Street. This location soon became overcrowded, and a committee headed by Howard began to look for a permanent location for the university. A 150-acre farm on the hill where the university now stands was selected, but the owner would only sell the farm in its entirety. So, all 150 acres were bought for $1,000 per acre with the help of the Freedmen's Bureau. All but 60 acres were immediately divided into lots and sold for a profit. In 1884, the federal government bought approximately 40 acres for a city reservoir now known as McMillan Reservoir Park, reducing the campus to its present 20 acres.

The first buildings erected were the Main Building, the Medical Department Building and hospital and the dormitories, along with a residence for O.O. Howard. The first dormitory erected was Miner Hall, named in honor of Myrtilla Miner, the founder of Porter's alma mater Miner Normal School. (In addition, a Miner Fund of $31,000 had been given to the university.) This would become the dormitory for women. A second dormitory, which would become the dormitory for men, was named Clark Hall in honor of David Clark, who contributed $25,000 to the university. Spaulding Hall, named in honor of Martha Spaulding, who bequeathed an estate to the university valued at $20,000, soon followed to relieve overcrowding in the Main Building and to house the Normal Department.

Other buildings erected before 1926 include the residence of James B. Johnson, one of the university's original trustees and administrators, which became known as Johnson Hall and later housed the Conservatory of Music, the School of Religion and the School of Social Work; the residence of university president Jeremiah E. Rankin, which was used as the home for the presidents until 1960; Andrew Rankin Memorial Chapel, named for Jeremiah's brother and whose widow contributed a large portion of the building funds; Freedmen's Hospital, built by the Freedmen's Bureau; Thirkield Science Hall, named for the university president who played a pivotal role in securing money from Congress to fund its building; and the Carnegie Library, built primarily with funds from businessman and philanthropist Andrew Carnegie.

The General Education Board and the Rosenwald Fund also provided grants to build the library at the cost of $50,000, a considerable sum in that day. Opened in 1910, this is the library where Porter would study and work as a student assistant and, later, as supervisor of the Negro Collection before the 1939 opening of Founders Library.

HOWARD UNIVERSITY LIBRARY BEFORE 1910

On April 8, 1867, at the second meeting of the board of trustees and before the university opened for classes, a committee was appointed to select books for a library. The committee was encouraged by a gift of twenty-five dollars from James C. Strout, the assistant librarian at the Library of Congress. Danford B. Nichols, a trustee and member of the executive committee, was appointed to the position of librarian and "entered upon the work with enthusiasm," notes Dyson. But Nichols was simultaneously the chairman of the Committee on Agriculture, professor in the Theological Department and chaplain of Freedmen's Hospital, leaving him with a limited amount of time and energy to devote to the library. Nichols resigned as librarian in 1873, and for the next twenty-five years (including 1875 to 1882, when it was seemingly vacant), it would remain a part-time position for approximately five professors or administrators.

The library's resources came from a variety of places—many of the trustees, including O.O. Howard, donated books and other materials. In 1868, $70 was allocated for the purchase of books. In 1869, Nichols sold his private library of 1,500 volumes to the university for $1,200. Also that year, John Williams of the Royal Shakespeare Society of England donated a set of the complete works of Shakespeare.

One of the university's most cherished acquisitions was the 1873 bequest of Lewis Tappan, a well-known abolitionist and one of the founders of the American Missionary Movement. His collection of approximately 1,650 items included books, periodicals, pamphlets, manuscripts, letters, pictures and clippings. This gift would become a valuable part of the Negro Collection.

In 1879, the board of trustees appropriated $3,000 for the purchase of library materials. In 1885, the federal government began appropriations for the purchase of books that ranged from $900 to $1,500 annually, as well as a separate appropriation for the law school library. And in 1890, the federal government authorized the Library of Congress and other agencies to send their duplicate copies to the university's library.

In 1900, John Wesley Cromwell, a formerly enslaved person, alumnus and well-known educator, editor, historian and lawyer, donated his collection of approximately seventy bound volumes of newspaper clippings. Another important donation prior to 1914 was that of black inventor William A. Lavalette, who donated sixty volumes of miscellaneous materials on African Americans.

However, the library's acquisitions were not easily accessed and were underutilized. As Dyson observes, "For many years most of the books in the library were useless…While many of the books were unfit for the pupils, others were useless because they were not catalogued and because the library was closed most of the day." For decades, the library was open only Monday through Friday from 2:00 p.m. to 4:00 p.m. under the auspices of student assistants, who also were responsible for cataloging the materials.

In addition, the location of the library was problematic. When the university opened, the library was situated in a small room in the building at Georgia Avenue. When the Main Building was erected, the library was moved to two or three rooms on the third floor, where it would stay from 1871 to 1910. Logan notes, "Climbing three flights of stairs to seek books from inadequately trained librarians and to read them in cramped rooms during the few hours a day when the library was open probably diminished the enthusiasm of all except the most earnest students."

For more than four decades, the university asked Congress for money for a library building. These requests took various forms—including those of a separate building, a combined library and chapel, shelving to convert the basement of the Andrew Rankin Chapel into a library and a large building in which a library, gymnasium and YMCA would be combined—all to no avail.

However, Howard University students and faculty were welcomed at the Library of Congress with its unmatched resources, thanks to the work of Librarian of Congress Ainsworth S. Spofford, who served from 1864 to 1897. Spofford transformed a small reference library into a national institution largely through the Copyright Act of 1870, which centralized all U.S. copyright registration and deposit activities at the Library of Congress and brought books, pamphlets, maps, prints, photographs and music into the institution without cost.

Howard University Library: 1910–26

The webpage on the history of the university's Founders Library states:

> *In 1910, the modern era began for Howard University's library functions when it occupied the Carnegie Library...Its opening marked the university's realization that the library must be a driving force in its academic development... With the opening of Carnegie Library, the professionalism and the size of the library staff grew in proportion to the size of the university's collection and its burgeoning enrollment. By 1924, the university's holdings had grown to more than 40,000 volumes through yearly appropriations for acquisitions of between $3,000 and $4,000, a sizable sum indicative of the university's expanding intellectual stature. The Carnegie Library building has remained an elegant presence on the Howard University quadrangle...*

In 1898, the board of trustees appointed Flora L.P. Johnson to the position of librarian. And while the board's decision might have been influenced by the fact that Johnson's father was a founder, trustee and treasurer of the university who offered her services for half the salary, she served quite ably until 1912. Johnson initiated classes in library economy, transferred the law library to the Law Building and hired two full-time staff members—Lulu E. Connors and Lulu V. Allan (who left the university in 1920 to become the librarian at the Miner Normal School, where she mentored Porter and encouraged her to become a librarian). Johnson also helped to facilitate the program for the dedication of the Carnegie Library. Held on April 25, 1910, the Carnegie Library dedication was a momentous event for the university with speeches by President William Howard Taft, Librarian of Congress Hebert Putnam and Andrew Carnegie. It also ushered in an era of greater appreciation for the role of a university library and the need for an adequate and well-trained staff.

Kelly Miller, an alumnus, professor of mathematics and sociology, dean of the College of Arts and Sciences and seminal figure in Howard University's history. *Moorland-Spingarn Research Center, Manuscript Division, Howard University.*

Also in 1910, Kelly Miller, an alumnus, professor of mathematics and sociology, dean of the College of Arts and Sciences and seminal figure in the university's history, proposed that a National Negro Library and Museum be established on the campus. The idea received a cool reception from the university's administrators, but Miller would not be easily deterred and would pursue the idea for the rest of his life. And for the immediate future, he sought to persuade his friend Jesse E. Moorland, an alumnus, trustee, clergyman and YMCA executive, to donate his extraordinary private collection of materials by and about Africans and African Americans to the university. The collection included more than three thousand titles: books, pamphlets, manuscripts, pictures and other items.

In 1912, Grace Liscom Watkins, a graduate of the Simmons College Library School, was hired as librarian and director of the Library School. She would serve until 1916 and preside over the acquisition of the Moorland Collection that Porter would come to supervise, grow and make world famous.

The January 1916 edition of the *Howard University Record* is devoted to the acquisition of the Jesse E. Moorland Collection. Included are the letter of gift from Moorland to university president Stephen M. Newman, the resolution of the board of trustees, letters of support from a wide array of individuals, a description of the collection and the university's plans for the collection and excerpts from the librarian's annual report for 1914–15.

In his letter dated December 18, 1914, Moorland writes:

> *The Collection has been regarded by many experts as probably the largest and most complete yet gathered by a single individual. I have spent many years and considerable means in getting this collection together...I am giving this collection to the University because it is the one place in America where the largest and best library on this subject should be constructively established. It is also the place where our young people who have the scholarly instinct should have the privilege of a complete Reference Library on the subject.*

Moorland also commented that he expected the items "to be properly catalogued and placed in an appropriate alcove or room." And in a postscript, he adds that "the profound interest of my personal friend, Professor Kelly Miller, in the establishment of such a library at Howard University, has had much to do with my decision."

At the board of trustees meeting on February 5, 1915, Moorland's gift was enthusiastically accepted and turned over to the university's library. In addition, the board created The Moorland Foundation: A Library of Negro Life. The minutes of the meeting note:

> *President Newman stated that he and Dean Miller, who is very much interested in this line of work, had been considering the idea of making this collection a nucleus for a department of the Library with the intention of establishing a Chair in the University. In this connection Dean Miller had written a large number of persons asking what they thought would be the result if Howard University should undertake to establish such a department on a large scale, and had received a number of encouraging replies.*

The replies came as letters of endorsement from library leaders (including Librarian of Congress Herbert Putnam; Ernest D. Burton, director of libraries at the University of Chicago; J.C. Schwab, librarian at Yale University; and Frederick C. Hicks, assistant librarian at Columbia University), those in academia (including Albert Bushnell Hart, professor of history at Harvard University; Arthur Hadley, president of Yale University; Franklin H. Giddings, professor of sociology at Columbia University; Herbert D. Foster, professor of history at Dartmouth College; and Francis G. Peabody, former professor and dean of Harvard's Divinity School), influential editors and publications (including W.E.B. Du Bois, editor of *The Crisis*; Ray Stannard

Jesse E. Moorland donated his collection to Howard University in 1914. *Moorland-Spingarn Research Center, Manuscript Division, Howard University.*

Baker, editor of *The American Magazine*; the *Christian Science Monitor*; and the *Springfield Daily Republican*) and other prominent individuals (including David H. Greer, bishop of the Diocese of New York, and Walter H. Page, U.S. ambassador to England).

The article in the *Howard University Record* also notes that the Tappan Collection, the Lavalette Collection, the Cromwell Collection and 260 volumes and many pamphlets scattered throughout the library were added to the Moorland Foundation, bringing the total to 1,500 volumes and many pamphlets. There were also plans to add material from magazines to the collection as well. The article observes, "It will be seen that the work of preparing this material for us is a large one. No library in the country has a classification suitable for our purpose. Hence one must be created...the entire collection will be put under the letter M (Moorland) and the necessary call numbers for the different kinds of literature will be attached to this letter." Lulu Allan was charged with classifying the material, Edith Brown (a recent graduate of Simmons College Library School) was hired as the library's cataloguer and Rose Hershaw was tasked with assisting her.

The growing importance of the university library in general is highlighted in Grace Watkins's annual report for 1914–15. A branch library was established for the School of Medicine, 2,172 books (including the Moorland Collection) were added to the library's holdings, 2,462 volumes were now catalogued and circulation statistics for the year stood at 29,897.

In 1916, Edward Christopher Williams was hired to replace Watkins as the university's librarian and director of the Library School, as well as professor of German and romance languages. A graduate of Adelbert College of Case Western Reserve University and the New York State Library School in Albany, Williams had taught library science courses at the Case Western Reserve Library School, served as principal of Washington's M Street High School (later renamed Dunbar High School) and, during his tenure at Howard University, would publish plays, poems, short stories and articles. Also, while serving at the university, he worked during the summer recesses at the 135th Street Branch Library in the Division of Negro Literature, History and Prints. Porter later recalled in her essay "Fifty Years of Collecting": "Edward Christopher Williams, the most scholarly librarian I have ever known, was the chief librarian at Howard University when I entered as a student...He was also a handsome, dapper, and very likeable man. He introduced me to many works of Negro authorship, as well as to figures like Dante, Queen Victoria, and Benvenuto Cellini. I was not only a student in his Italian class but a student assistant in the library." She also noted that everyone called him "E.C."

Porter enrolled in Howard University only weeks after Mordecai W. Johnson assumed the presidency on September 1, 1926. The thirty-six-year-old ordained Baptist minister was at that time serving as pastor of the First Baptist Church in Charleston, West Virginia. He held BA (Bachelor of Arts) degrees from Atlanta Baptist College (now Morehouse College) and the University of Chicago, a Bachelor of Divinity degree from Rochester Theological Seminary and a Master of Sacred Theology degree from Harvard University.

When Johnson became the university's first African American president, there were eight schools and colleges that lacked national accreditation, 1,700 students and a budget of $700,000. When he retired thirty-four years later, there were ten schools and colleges, all fully accredited; graduate programs with the authority to grant the PhD degree; 6,000 students; a budget of $8 million; twenty new buildings; and a faculty that included some of the most well-known African American scholars.

When Porter arrived on campus in September 1926, she was able to transfer credits from both Miner Normal School and Columbia University, enabling her to earn her BA degree in approximately two years. In an interview with Harriet Jackson Scarupa for an article in the January 1990 issue of *New Directions: The Howard University Magazine*, Porter revealed that her main goal was to earn her degree "and get through as soon as possible." But she also fondly remembered "such Howard legends as Alain Locke, Sterling Brown and Benjamin Brawley, who were not only her teachers but

Mordecai W. Johnson, the first African American president of
Howard University, served from 1926 to 1960. *Moorland-Spingarn
Research Center, Manuscript Division, Howard University.*

became her friends...Another attraction of the university for her was a
young art teacher named James Porter, whom she initially met on one of her
summer sojourns to New York" and would later marry.

While studying at Howard, Porter attended the Columbia University
library school summer sessions and worked at the 135th Street Branch

Library with Edward Christopher Williams. In the summer of 1928, the year in which she earned her BA degree from Howard, she was working at the library when Williams offered her a full-time professional job at the university. In a 1993 interview with Avril Johnson Madison, Porter recalled: "I remember him coming down the steps lickety-split from the second floor, and he said, 'Oh, Miss Rose wants you to take a job here, and I want you to come to Howard.' I said, 'You haven't offered me a job at Howard.' He said, 'Well, I'm offering it to you now.' So I came back to Howard instead of staying up in New York City."

Later that year, Porter moved permanently to the District of Columbia to begin her duties as a cataloguer in the university's Carnegie Library.

Chapter 3

COLLECTING AND ORGANIZING AFRICANA MATERIALS AT HOWARD UNIVERSITY

The Moorland Foundation was formally opened on October 1, 1932. In order to publicize the collection, a notice about the resources and the hours of operation was put in the Howard University catalogue of classes. To further publicize the Moorland Foundation, Porter prepared lists of recent acquisitions, a biographical booklet on important blacks, posters, broadsides and exhibits.

One of her major decisions was how to make Africana materials more easily accessible to patrons looking for resources in the card catalogue. She decided to modify the Dewey decimal classification system. According to Porter in her interview with Harriet Jackson Scarupa, the Dewey decimal system had no way to accommodate books dealing with the black experience. She was outraged by the fact that there were only two categories in which to place the rich Africana experience, so she devised her own classification scheme. She explained to Scarupa:

> *Under the system, everything related to the Negro was classified under "325," which was the number for "colonization," or "326," which was the number for "slavery." The woman in charge of the Dewey decimal classification at Howard couldn't see why I didn't want to put a book of poetry by James Weldon Johnson under "325" or "326"—which was ridiculous. I just began to base everything about Black literature and history wherever it fell in the regular Dewey decimal classification—if it were a book on Blacks in the Revolutionary War, it would go under the same*

Dorothy Porter at her desk in the Carnegie Library, Howard University. *Moorland-Spingarn Research Center, Manuscript Division, Howard University.*

> *number as "Revolutionary War" for instance. It was very simple, you see, very simple.*

Thomas C. Battle, retired director of the Moorland-Spingarn Research Center, wrote in a biographical sketch in the *Dictionary of American Library Biography* (2003), "Wesley used subject headings more appropriate to describing the black experience well before such terms came into more common usage and were incorporated into classifications schemes."

COLLECTION DEVELOPMENT, 1932–42

During its first decade, the use of the Moorland Foundation increased each year; however, funding did not keep up with the increasing demands and the need to develop the collections. Porter reported on her collection development efforts in each annual report.

Porter reported that several special projects were undertaken during the 1931–32 year, a re-cataloguing of the entire collection (books, pamphlets, periodicals and clippings), indexing of important materials found in periodicals not previously indexed in any periodical index, the development of a classification scheme whereby the books could be logically arranged on the shelves, the development of a card index for limited materials about blacks not readily accessible and the development of authority lists to organize the library catalogue and bibliographical information on black authors.

Class assignments were a driving force in developing the collection. Porter wrote in her 1932 annual report:

> *Perhaps the greatest interest in the collection and in Negro literature has been Dr. Brawley's course in Negro literature offered this spring quarter. The majority of his students have spent 3 to 4 hours daily on his assigned readings. Great interest was placed on the rarity and value of the books by Dr. Brawley. The students were unusually careful with them and have taken great pride in the fact that they were permitted to use these books...A distinction must be made between those books which are rare and out-of-print and those which may be duplicated and used for general reference.*

Benjamin Brawley was chair of the English Department. Several of his books were considered standard college text, including *The Negro in Literature and Art in the United States* (1918).

In her 1938–39 report, Porter wrote:

> *These demands [on the collection] are indicative, of course, of two things: increased research in the field of the Negro and additional effort on the part of the general [public] and agencies serving its needs to get information on various aspects of Negro life. There is ample evidence to show that these demands will soon compel us to initiate more specialized development of the collection. We certainly must not allow the requests for particular information to exceed unreasonably the resources of the collection. Certain standards can be maintained only if there is wise anticipation of the needs of scholarship and lay inquiry. Within this problem are comprehended those of adequate professional and clerical assistance within the department and of a proportional purchase fund for needed books and materials. If the collection is to be administered efficiently and if it's various sections are to be enriched and made increasingly attractive to scholars, then these practical considerations will have to be dealt with within a very short space of time.*

NATIONAL NEGRO LIBRARY AND MUSEUM

After Moorland's initial gift in 1914, Kelly Miller continued to work on his 1910 proposal for a National Negro Library and Museum on the campus of Howard University. In his numerous articles and essays published in major magazines and newspapers, including the *Baltimore Afro American* and the *Washington Tribune*, he lobbied nonstop for the museum. Miller sent these essays and articles to a wide array of people and organizations, including alumni and members of the Howard University Board of Trustees. He solicited others to also write letters of support.

In a July 18, 1938 letter to North Carolina Agricultural and Technical College president F.D. Bluford, Miller wrote, "Here is a proposit on which the united effort of Trustees, Administration, Faculty, Alumni, Student Body and Well Wishers can push on to the top and make our beloved Alma Mater in truth and in deed the 'Capstone of Negro Education.'"

In an August 1, 1938 letter to the president of the Howard University Board of Trustees, T.L. Hungate, Miller estimated the cost of establishing this museum. He wrote:

> As to the cost of the undertaking, only expert opinion can have any great value on this point. From my general judgment gathered from the appraisement of several individual collections reinforced by consultation with experienced librarians, I feel certain that it would require as much as two hundred and fifty thousand dollars ($250,000) to get the enterprise well under way...My judgment is that the University should immediately appoint an expert to make a preliminary survey of the field and determine the feasibility as well as the probable cost. The essential thing is that Howard University, at once adopt and sponsor the idea.

Miller then asked Charles H. Wesley, a Howard University professor of history, to serve as this expert. In that same August 1, 1938 letter to Hungate, Miller noted:

> Mr. Edwin C. Embree, President of the Rosenwald Foundation, along with many others with whom I have corresponded, expressed their view that Congress might be induced to supply the necessary funds if the matter is competently and justifiably presented. There are several outstanding private collections which should sooner or later find their way in this master library, either by purchase, gift, or legacy.

In an August 6, 1938 article in the *New York Amsterdam News*, Miller wrote:

> *The purpose of this museum is to promote social knowledge by way of research scholarship in a field of great interest and importance for all students of social inquiry regardless of race or color. In this way, Howard University would make itself the center of attraction to all those who are in quest of information in this field.*

Porter was appointed to the faculty committee on the National Negro Library and Museum that held its initial meeting on September 20, 1938, "to consider a statement to be sent to the University president and Board of Trustees their recommendations for the museum."

When the board of trustees met on October 25, 1938, it voted to approve the proposed museum. The minutes of the meeting noted:

> *1. That the Board approve the general idea of the National Negro Library and Museum as outlined by the special Faculty Committee in its report of October 11, 1938;*
>
> *2. That the Administration be instructed to proceed with such steps as will bring about the full realization of the National Negro Library and Museum project as rapidly as possible;*
>
> *3. That priority be given to the acquisition of collections of books, documents and other articles which may be lost to Howard University through further delay;*
>
> *4. That the Board express to the Special Faculty Committee on the National Negro Library and Museum project its appreciation for its constructive suggestions, and to Dr. Kelly Miller in particular its appreciation for his long continued espousal of this cause.*

Despite the best efforts of Miller and others, the museum proposal stalled, and it would not come to fruition until 1973, some thirty-four years after Miller's death in 1939.

COLLECTION DEVELOPMENT, 1943–53

In accessing Africana collections during this time period, Arna Bontemps wrote in his article "Special Collections of Negroana," published in *The Library Quarterly* (July 1944):

The distinguishing feature of this collection is its relation to the curriculum of the university. Its growth and expansion have been, in the opinion of its director, basically conditioned by Howard courses in the various aspects on Negro life, literature, and history. The Moorland Foundation, like the collections at Fisk, Atlanta, and other colored schools, includes everything about the Negro which promises to fit into the educational program of the institution...The materials viewed as a spectrum might show rarities on one end and at the other the titles of "Howardiana," including the writings of Howard faculty members, materials about the university, and the university's own publications...The influence of the Moorland Room had been considerable.

Requests for information increased each year as high school students, doctoral candidates, freelance writers, editors, book dealers and others asked for assistance. Requests came from every state and from overseas locations such as Germany, England, Belgium, Korea, Japan, South Africa and other countries. These requests came via letter, telephone and in person.

COLLECTION DEVELOPMENT, 1954–64

During this decade, Porter wrote to several universities, publishers, government agencies and African research centers in England and Africa, including the International African Institute and the University College at Ibadan (Nigeria), successfully soliciting materials. She noted: "We wish to obtain as many works as possible relating to the various African peoples, especially books and pamphlets written by Africans. Will you kindly send us any of your publications which are gratis or exchange items? We shall be especially grateful for the names of African authors and their publications."

Porter also focused on acquiring African newspapers. African students especially enjoyed reading newspapers from their home countries. Sometimes the Moorland Foundation held the only collection of these papers outside of the Library of Congress.

In reflecting on the growth of the collection to date, Porter observed:

Three decades have passed since the Negro Collection came into organized existence. It has been four and one-half decades since Dr. Jesse E. Moorland presented his private library of some 3,000 books about the Negro—a collection which he hoped would serve as a firm foundation for a truly useful research library. The Collection enriched in gifts and purchases has grown into a research library engaging in numerous different activities related to the collecting, preservation and servicing of varied materials which record the life and history of the Negro people everywhere. The primary aim of the Negro Collection has been to serve Howard University students, faculty and administrative offices, but more and more it has been a definite responsibility to scholars, research workers and the general public. These responsibilities are increasing as Africana area programs develop in colleges and universities throughout the country and major research projects get underway in various places. Increased interest in the Negro by white students has increased our circulation statistics.

COLLECTION DEVELOPMENT, 1965–73

On May 24, 1966, Porter wrote a letter to the National Arts and Humanities Foundation (composed of two autonomous units, the National Endowment for the Arts and the National Endowment for the Humanities) in Washington, D.C., asking for support for the publication of "certain bibliographical projects which have been devised to assist the growth and greater usefulness of the Negro Collection at Howard University, and to launch other bibliographical projects with a view to rendering the greatest possible aid and service to students and scholars using our collection who must rely heavily on bibliographical assistance in the course of their research."

Porter also included with this letter a detailed summary of her annual reports from 1939 forward on the needs and recommendations to improve services in the Moorland Foundation. In the last paragraph of this report, Porter proclaimed: "Future development of the Negro Collection depends on funds and staff. Howard University could become a bibliographical center for African and Negro Studies...Several centers of African Studies periodically circulate lists of their African acquisitions. Howard University is expected to do the same."

Porter launched microfilming projects for the shelflist cards for both the Moorland and Spingarn catalogues along with a G.K. Hall project to microfilm the Moorland and Spingarn dictionary catalogues. With the G.K. Hall project, thousands of cards were corrected and hundreds retyped.

Participants in the seminar sponsored by the Ford Foundation for Black Studies directors, Aspen, Colorado, 1970. *JWJ MSS 93. Dorothy Porter Wesley Papers, James Weldon Johnson Collection in the Yale Collection of American Literature, Beinecke Rare Book and Manuscript Library.*

Porter was invited to attend a July 1970 seminar on black studies held in Aspen, Colorado, and co-sponsored by the Ford Foundation and the Academy for Educational Development. Historian Edgar Toppin wrote in a May 15, 1970 letter on behalf of the academy, "This will be a welcome opportunity to share in exploring the achievements, problems and prospects of black studies programs."

Howard University was subsequently one of the recipients of a Ford Foundation grant. Porter reported that the grant

> *enabled us to inventory and catalog or index a large proportion of unprocessed manuscripts, tapes, phono-recordings, pamphlets, periodicals, newspapers, pictorial representations and ephemera. Hundreds of issues of periodicals and newspapers which were becoming unusable because they were too brittle to handle without breaking were microfilmed or xeroxed. The Ford grant made possible further organization of the collection as a whole as well as permitted us to considerably expand on early drafts of a*

manual of procedures necessary as a guideline for our growing staff. We are most appreciative of the support and interest of the Ford Foundation.

In recognizing the support of the Ford Foundation, the 2007 report *Inclusive Scholarship: Developing Black Studies in the United States; A 25ᵗʰ Anniversary Retrospective of Ford Foundation Grants, 1982–2007,* noted:

> *Beginning in 1969 and throughout the next decade, Ford Foundation program officer James Scanlon would make a number of grants to help sustain African American Studies programs at historically Black colleges and universities (HBCUs), as well as at predominantly white institutions. Grants for Black Studies initiatives at HBCUs were made to Fisk, Howard, and Lincoln Universities; Morgan State College; and the Atlanta University Center.*

Porter was also enthusiastic about the indexing of *Opportunity Magazine* and the completion of the G.K. Hall publications: the Jesse Edward Moorland Collection of Negro Life and History and the Arthur B. Spingarn Collection of Negro Authors. G.K. Hall sent three sets of these dictionary catalogues as gifts for the collection. She again stressed in her annual reports the need to "study ways in which we can use computers for the compilation as well as for the use of storage banks of bibliographical information." Porter reported that holdings in the Moorland Foundation had increased to 180,343 items and that a large number of books, pamphlets and manuscripts needed to be processed. In addition, ninety-four reels of newspapers had been microfilmed, along with the Marian Anderson clippings and the records of the Woodlawn Cemetery in Washington, D.C.

Classroom assignments continued to be an important part of collection development. For example, during the Howard University centennial year of 1967, special assignments were given to students to research various aspects on the history of the university.

ACQUISITIONS (GIFTS AND PURCHASES), 1932–42

To supplement her meager acquisitions budget, Porter appealed to faculty to donate manuscripts of their published works as well as any letters from noted individuals. She also asked that they order duplicate copies of books pertaining to blacks so that one copy could be donated to the Moorland Foundation and, if possible, an additional copy to the Carnegie Library for circulation. In addition, she appealed to publishers, authors and friends who were collectors to donate their materials. She also rummaged through the attics and basements of recently deceased persons to acquire materials.

As more black scholars joined the faculty of Howard University, interest in topics related to persons of African descent increased in the fields of history, sociology, literature and philosophy. To meet this demand, Porter worked hard to provide the needed resources in the Moorland Foundation. She often spoke of how difficult this was without an adequate acquisitions budget. Fortunately, Jesse E. Moorland continued to donate books to the collection.

In Porter's 1935–36 annual report, she wrote:

> *The growth of the collection is still too slow when compared to the current demands on the collection. It is obvious that the lack of funds for the purchase of materials greatly handicaps research activity. The acquisition of special collections and course materials so frequently associated with scholarly investigations is impossible unless money for the purchase of these materials is available...The library is embarrassed when it is unable to answer reference questions because tools are not in the collection.*

Always on the lookout for materials for the Moorland Foundation, in the early 1940s, Porter visited book dealers in New York and, while there, also visited the home of collector Arthur B. Spingarn to view his vast private collection of Africana books. She hoped to secure his collection for the Moorland Foundation. Also during this period, she received valuable materials such as the papers of lawyer Charles H. Houston and additions to the John Wesley Cromwell Collection.

Acquisitions (Gifts and Purchases), 1943–53

Arthur B. Spingarn Collection

The year 1946 was a banner year for acquiring collections. Porter was successful in purchasing the Arthur B. Spingarn Collection of Negro Authors. Spingarn was a lawyer and NAACP official. An article covering the official opening of the Spingarn Collection was published in the

Right: Arthur B. Spingarn developed a collection of works by black authors that was unique in its depth, breadth and quality. *Moorland-Spingarn Research Center, Manuscript Division, Howard University.*

Below: Dedication of the Arthur B. Spingarn Collection at the Moorland Foundation, Founders Library, Howard University, 1946. *Moorland-Spingarn Research Center, Manuscript Division, Howard University.*

December 1948 issue of the *Howard University Bulletin*. Titled "Howard University Acquires the Most Comprehensive Collection of Works by Negro Authors in the World," the article cited the importance of this collection, as emphasized by Howard president Mordecai Johnson in the following statement:

Dr. Arthur B. Spingarn has greatly honored Howard University in allowing us to acquire his distinguished collection of books by Negro authors. This collection is, without doubt, the most comprehensive and interesting group of books by Negroes ever collected in the world. Howard University rejoices to place at the disposal of students, scholars and writers the richness and diversity of these cultural materials.

According to the article, the Moorland Foundation was "now the largest and the most valuable research library in America for the study of Negro life and history." The article also noted several of the unique documents in this collection. Among them are:

Particularly strong coverage of Afro-Cuban, Afro-Brazilian, and Haitian writers.

Notable was the large number of native African writers represented and items in many African languages.

Other languages in the collection were Arabic, German, Dutch, Portuguese, Russian, Latin, Creole, Spanish and French.

Many of the writers were unknown to American scholars and their writings could serve to open up new and profitable fields for the American literary historian and creative artist.

Several hundred slave narratives and autobiographies which give first-hand descriptions of the customs and practices of slave life.

Many rare editions of works by Negro authors, including early American leaders and writers. Their works are indispensable for students of early Negro literature and history.

Rich in works by British and French West Indian, Cuban, Central and South American writers of color.

Institutional reports and publications of various Negro social, political and religious groups.

Proceedings and minutes of historical political and "race" conventions.

Ephemeral pieces such as newspapers, announcements, invitations, circulars, theater bills, mimeographed letters, and pictures.

Also in 1946, Beatrice M. Gardiner, the widow of historian and postal worker Leon Gardiner, donated twenty-five boxes of books and pamphlets on blacks in Philadelphia.

ACQUISITIONS (GIFTS AND PURCHASES), 1954–64

Gifts included books and periodicals, some of which completed serial runs. Porter observed that as manuscript and illustrative materials were added, "It became more and more apparent that much of the history of the Negro is yet to be written. In this material are to be found rich opportunities for original research, as was indicated by scholars who found our still uncalendered manuscripts of lively interest."

As she gave a glowing report on the gifts that were coming in, she also bemoaned the fact that gifts were not readily made available due to a lack of staff. She wrote: "It is regrettable that gift additions cannot be readied for accessioning and accessioned within the year of their arrival for a true picture of our annual growth cannot be discerned in our present annual accession record. Numerous items received as gifts are not accessioned until several years after their arrival. This situation should be remedied."

To draw further attention to the need to have gifts accessioned, Porter noted: "Eight boxes of items relating to [noted heart surgeon and hospital founder] Daniel Hale Williams donated more than a year ago have only been unpacked and placed in filing cabinets. The [surgeon] Louis T. Wright Collection of Writings By and About the Negro Physician remained boxed more than a year and was only unpacked this spring."

Faculty continued to donate materials. Walter Dyson donated the materials he used in his history on Howard University, including Howard periodicals, university catalogues and the manuscript in all its stages (typed copy, galley and page proofs). After Dyson's death, his widow, Mary, donated supplemental books, periodicals, pamphlets and manuscripts related to the history of Howard University.

James Porter gave Daumier prints that were caricatures of black life. Mordecai Johnson sent pamphlets, reports, periodicals and annual reports from various Howard University divisions.

Arthur B. Spingarn continued to give materials to the Moorland Foundation, including books, periodicals, reports, addresses and programs. He donated the first draft of W.E.B. Du Bois's *Philadelphia Negro*. He also donated Swedish, Finnish and Norwegian translations of books by South African novelist Peter Abrahams and well-known author Richard Wright. In addition, Spingarn augmented the collection with newspaper clippings, manuscripts and correspondence related to his brother, Joel E. Spingarn, an educator and NAACP official.

Porter believed that if it had not been for the gifts from donors, alumni and friends, the collection could not have survived. One of the major gifts was the collection of papers and books of lawyer, writer and intellectual Archibald Grimké, which had been in storage for thirty years. Some 12,000 manuscripts were in this collection, along with more than 473 books, 377 pamphlets and 120 periodicals. Also, Maria Brown Frazier, widow of famed sociologist E. Franklin Frazier, donated her late husband's papers.

Another important gift collection was that of John Hope, former Morehouse College president. Included were eight hundred letters, speeches, pamphlets, periodicals, photos and miscellaneous items from the years 1894 to 1936.

More than eight thousand items from the Works Progress Administration (WPA), including letters, reports of the director, periodicals, programs and photos, were gifted to the Moorland Foundation.

South Carolina judge J. Waites Waring gave seven albums of letters, newspaper articles, circulars, etc. on the civil rights movement from 1960 to 1964. These were added to his collection previously donated five years earlier. Another valuable donation was that of Mable Staupers, executive secretary of National Association of Colored Graduate Nurses (NACGN), who gave 188 items relating to that organization.

The Moorland Foundation purchased microfilm copies of black newspapers such as the *California Eagle, Chicago Defender, Pittsburgh Courier* and *Norfolk Journal and Guide*. It also purchased the *Southern Workman*, published by Hampton Institute (now Hampton University). In addition, the foundation was able to purchase two very important publications—the Catalog of the Schomburg Collection in the New York Public Library and the Catalog of the African Collection at Northwestern University.

The gem of gifts coming to the Moorland Foundation during this period was the Alain Leroy Locke Collection. Locke is best known as a theorist, critic and interpreter of African American literature and art and is considered by many to be the "Father of the Harlem Renaissance" for his 1925 publication *The New Negro: An Interpretation*—an anthology of poetry, essays, plays, book reviews, photography, music, visual artistry and portraiture by white and black artists. This book was an expanded version of his March 1925 publication of a special issue of *Survey Graphic* titled "Harlem: Mecca of the Negro." His collection included more than 1,850 books in the fields of philosophy, religion, sociology, music, education, literature, art, economics, political science, language and African American history and literature. In Porter's article in *Black Bibliophiles and Collectors*, she remembered:

*He saved his books, every scrap of paper, thousands of manuscripts, photographs,
medical x-rays, ticket stubs, train schedules, gas bills, and countless notes taken
from almost any book or periodical to suit his research purposes. Locke even
kept fragile, deteriorated Christmas toys from his boyhood days. One object is a
large piece of old wood sent to Locke by Zora Neale Hurston, who claimed it
was from the helm of the last slave ship that arrived in Florida where she lived.
Locke had become a Baha'i before his death, and his collection of books on that
faith has been of interest to other local Baha'is. When future biographers of
Locke reconstruct his collecting activities, much about the man will be revealed.*

ACQUISITIONS (GIFTS AND PURCHASES), 1965–73

The Moorland Foundation policy for purchases continued to be all books by
black authors, funds permitting. Noteworthy were additions in the area of
Portuguese and French African studies.

Amy Spingarn, the widow of Joel E. Spingarn, gave seventy-one letters
received from Joel and her daughter Hope. Many of the letters from Joel
were related to the NAACP and its 1912 convention. The letters were not to
be used without permission for twenty-five years.

During this decade, Arthur Spingarn donated an impressive array of
books, pamphlets and manuscripts. Included were some forty-five manuscript
letters from well-known individuals, including Frederick Douglass, Toussaint
L'Ouverture, Henry O. Tanner, Claude McKay and Charles W. Chesnutt.

Records of the Washington Conservatory of Music were donated by
Geneva Turner, the spouse of educator and linguist Lorenzo Dow Turner.
She also donated the conservatory's constitution and bylaws, meeting
minutes, a checkbook and a scrapbook.

In February 1967, Peter Marshall Murray, a graduate of the Howard
University Medical School and former member of the board of trustees,
donated his collection of personal papers, photographs, articles, speeches
and radio and television scripts, as well as his memoir and reports to the
medical boards, medical societies and medical schools. Porter was delighted
because this collection would be of great value to the scholar studying blacks
in medicine, particularly the integration of black doctors in hospitals.

Materials came in from the John F. Cook family, one of the richest families in
the District of Columbia. The donation included personal papers, photographs,
diplomas, badges and medals. Documents also came in on Sissieretta Jones,

the famous soprano, and Constance McLaughlin Green, author of books on Washington, D.C. history, donated materials used to research her books.

Porter felt that the most significant gift to the collection during this decade was from the libraries of James Monroe Gregory, Eugene Monroe Gregory and Thomas Monroe Gregory. The Gregory family represented six generations of achievement in the black community. James Monroe Gregory was instrumental in securing the first appropriation for Howard University ($10,000). For years, he was considered the leading exponent of higher education for blacks in the District of Columbia.

The Howardiana Collection continued to grow as more and more faculty donated materials and more than eighty-five alumni donated more than five hundred items related to the university.

Also in the area of acquisitions, Porter noted that materials from the Caribbean had not been given a high priority. However, a collection of specialized materials on the Caribbean had been purchased. She noted that there were courses now being taught on Haitian literature and drama, and she planned to acquire materials on Haiti as they became available.

The Library of Congress had duplicate cards from the Daniel A.P. Murray Collection sent to Porter so that she could check them against holdings in the Moorland Foundation. Murray was an assistant librarian at the Library of Congress from 1871 to 1925. Duplicate holdings from his collection were later transferred to the Moorland Foundation.

Both Arno Press and University Microfilms gave reprints of microfilm reels of materials supplied to them from the Moorland Foundation for duplication. In addition, microfilm copies of African and African American titles were also purchased. Several embassies, including Ghana, Senegal, Sierra Leone, Tanzania, Somali, Madagascar, Guyana and the U.S. Virgin Islands, also donated materials.

During this decade, a number of manuscript collections were received, including those of clergyman and lawyer T. McCants Stewart, physician Charles R. Drew, educator Anna J. Cooper, historian Helen G. Edmonds and educator Charles Eaton Burch.

STAFFING

The Moorland Foundation's first decade began on an upbeat note, as Porter was able to employ Howard University student assistants, National Youth

Administration (NYA) students and Works Progress Administration (WPA) assistants to help with major projects. Both the NYA and WPA were part of President Franklin Roosevelt's New Deal program. The New Deal program came to an end in the early 1940s as the United States prepared to enter World War II. Subsequently, the Moorland Foundation suffered from low funding and inadequate staffing.

Porter continued to look for ways to increase and promote staff. In an October 21, 1958 letter to President Mordecai Johnson, she acknowledged pay raises but also inquired about merit increases. She stressed that her staff had

> *served in Founders Library for periods of from 18–31 years, three of us as professional librarians and supervisors, and one as secretary to the Director of Universities Libraries. At no time have we received monetary recognition for such services as is the custom in better industrial and educational institutions. Yet we have continued to give efficient and dependable service to promote the successful functioning of the Library and have sought to improve our professional status through study, travel and participation in professional organizations.*

With increased circulation, Porter felt that it left little time to acquire and effectively process materials or promote the resources through bibliographies. In short, she felt that the quality of services was suffering. The problem of overcrowding (stacks, work space, catalogue units and storage), low salaries and not enough staff was a real dilemma. On June 10, 1966, Porter wrote a letter to Joseph Reason, the university librarian, forecasting that "the shortsightedness of the administration in failing to provide minimum staff needs is regrettable and jeopardizes the future expansion of the collection."

In her 1966–67 annual report, an exasperated Porter wrote: "I recall to you my previous request for staff and equipment. I am at a loss to understand why no action has yet been taken to provide the same since they are vital to the servicing and development of the collection." She did note her appreciation for the hiring of graduate students as "stack attendants."

FACULTY RELATIONS

During her tenure, Porter served on many Howard University committees, including the Dean of Women's Committee, the Committee on Writing the History of Howard University, the Committee on University Objectives, the

Dorothy Porter at the retirement reception for Joseph Reason, director of the Howard University Library from 1946 to 1971. *Moorland-Spingarn Research Center, Manuscript Division, Howard University.*

Provisional Committee on Howard University Faculty Club and the Faculty Women's Committee on Student Creative Awards.

Many members of the faculty were working on books that required them to use the Moorland Foundation. English professors Sterling Brown and Arthur P. Davis were working on a new edition of *The Negro Caravan*. Professors Emmett Dorsey (political science) and E. Franklin Frazier (sociology) were also writing new books in their fields. Porter worked closely with university librarian Joseph Reason until his 1971 retirement.

Many documents coming into the collection were in foreign languages, and faculty members who were fluent in those languages were often asked to translate the documents.

VISITORS AND REQUESTS FOR INFORMATION

Each year, requests for information via letter, telephone and in person increased from Howard University students and faculty, students from other universities,

Dorothy Porter helping an unidentified student in the Moorland Foundation Reading Room, Founders Library, Howard University. *Moorland-Spingarn Research Center, Manuscript Division, Howard University.*

writers, editors, book dealers and the general public. Requests came from near and far, including New York, Florida, Kentucky, North Carolina, Ohio, Oregon, Texas and California. Researchers also came from Iran, Brazil, Australia, Chile, France, Thailand, Ecuador, Eritrea, England, Germany, Korea, Japan, Belgium, South Africa, the Caribbean and other areas. The U.S. State Department often sent visitors as well, including Haitian librarian Max Besant. The Moorland Foundation served as a liaison to the Hispanic Foundation, which requested assistance in locating Haitian poets and for materials for inclusion in the *Handbook of Latin American Studies*, published by the Library of Congress.

Many interlibrary loan requests came from abroad. Some materials were too fragile to send, so copies had to be made. Agencies requesting information included the Embassy of Japan; the Central Intelligence Agency (CIA); the U.S. Census Bureau; the Children's Hospital in Washington, D.C.; the Johnson Publishing Company; the U.S. Commission on Civil Rights; and many others. These requests required extensive searching as well as the preparation of bibliographies on the topics researched.

FOUNDERS LIBRARY

During the Moorland Foundation's first decade, use of the resources by faculty, students and researchers steadily increased. The Carnegie Library had also become inadequate for the rapidly growing collections and increased use by students and faculty, and plans were made for a new library building. Porter dedicated much time and effort on the planning committee for the new library.

This facility, under construction since 1929, opened in grand style in 1939 as Founders Library. Walter Dyson, in his history of the university, writes: "The Founders Library was named in honor of the 17 men who founded Howard and to whom the charter was issued. The cornerstone was laid on June 10, 1937, and it opened for service on January 3, 1939. On May 25, 1939, the Secretary of the Interior, Harold Ickes, presented the building to the University as a gift of the Federal Government."

The Moorland Foundation moved into Founders Library, where it enjoyed larger facilities for patrons and staff. Porter's work on the committee proved invaluable in securing this new space.

TRAVEL

During the 1930s and 1940s, Porter traveled to Cuba, Massachusetts, Pennsylvania and Connecticut, where she visited the Yale University Library. She continually requested travel funds to enable her to "locate, examine and arrange for the acquisition of materials of value to research which otherwise might not come to the library." Traveling to various collections to see what they owned and acquiring documents was most important to Porter. After trips to both Duke University and the University of North Carolina in the 1950s, she noted "the interest in Negro manuscripts on the part of both universities." She also visited the State Archives of North Carolina and the State Library of North Carolina.

On a subsequent trip to South America, Porter visited libraries, bookshops and cultural centers in Chile, Brazil, Uruguay, Argentina, Peru and Ecuador. Continuing her travels, Porter attended a conference titled "American Interest in Library Development Abroad," organized by the Peace Corp's Jamaica Training Program, to discuss Jamaican literature and Caribbean bibliographies.

During a 1961 trip to the eighth National Conference on Africa, sponsored by UNESCO, she acquired copies of speeches, pamphlets and bibliographies. Porter served as a rapporteur for the humanities panel "Africa and the United States: Images and Realities." The conference was attended by UNESCO and United Nations experts as well as prominent African political, educational and cultural leaders.

In her 1961 annual report, Porter discussed the value of attending conferences. She noted that the "information received relating to the development of Africana studies, bibliographical trends and Africana collections is of considerable help to us here. The benefit gained from persons working in similar collections is obvious. Attendance at meetings is a part of the professional experience."

Also in 1961, Porter, conducting personal research, went to Massachusetts to visit Boston University, Boston Public Library, Harvard University, Essex Institute, Smith College, the Salem Public Library and the Falmouth Historical Society.

One of the major highlights of this decade was the trip Porter took to West Africa in March 1962. She visited Ghana, Nigeria, the Ivory Coast and Senegal

National Library of Nigeria staff, Lagos, Nigeria, 1964. *JWJ MSS 93. Dorothy Porter Wesley Papers, James Weldon Johnson Collection in the Yale Collection of American Literature, Beinecke Rare Book and Manuscript Library.*

Dorothy Porter at Ford Foundation party in Lagos, Nigeria, with her husband, James A. Porter, 1964. *JWJ MSS 93. Dorothy Porter Wesley Papers, James Weldon Johnson Collection in the Yale Collection of American Literature, Beinecke Rare Book and Manuscript Library.*

Dorothy Porter at a conference on Négritude in Dakar, Senegal, 1971. *JWJ MSS 93. Dorothy Porter Wesley Papers, James Weldon Johnson Collection in the Yale Collection of American Literature, Beinecke Rare Book and Manuscript Library.*

to obtain materials for the growing Africa collections. She eventually acquired more than five hundred items and visited archives, cultural centers and libraries. Porter interviewed more than one hundred librarians while in Africa.

From 1962 to 1964, Porter was on leave on a Ford Foundation grant to work as an acquisitions librarian to help set up the National Library of Nigeria in Lagos. Upon her return to the Moorland Foundation, she brought books, pamphlets, periodicals, et cetera. She was also interviewed by the United States Information Agency (USIA), and her interview was broadcast throughout the world.

Porter returned to Dakar, Senegal, in April 1971 to attend a conference on Négritude, a literary and ideological movement developed by French-speaking black intellectuals in Africa and the Caribbean. While there, she was given some materials and also purchased books, periodicals and newspapers.

ACCOMPLISHMENTS

In 1936, Porter supervised a project titled "Research in Education in Universities," sponsored by the U.S. Office of Education. She also contributed to "A List of Publications Indicating the Educational Development of Howard University as an Institution of Higher Learning, 1861–1936." The final report for the project, titled *The Report on Educational Research Study*, was submitted in December of that year.

As her name became widely known for her knowledge about Africana resources, Porter was often asked to speak and participate in various activities. She spoke at schools (particularly during Negro History Week, now Black History Month), book clubs, churches and civic organizations. Among the projects in which she participated was one to bring about better library facilities for black students in junior high schools. Her speaking engagements also included an interview with the Voice of America on "Howard University and the Library on the Negro" that was broadcast in Africa and Asia. She also spoke on "The Legacy of Colonialism," to the D.C. League of Women Voters.

She published articles and book reviews in the *Journal of Negro History*, *American Scholar*, the *Negro History Bulletin* and the *National Educational Outlook Among Negroes*. She also contributed to the *Dictionary of American Biography*. Throughout her career, Porter contributed bibliographies to the *Journal of*

Negro Education. Dolores Leffall, who worked in the Moorland Foundation from the mid-1950s through the mid-1960s, compiled with Porter many of these bibliographies. In a June 17, 2014 telephone interview with Leffall, she said, "For the *Journal of Negro Education*, I also served as the book review editor while Porter served on their advisory board."

Porter increased her skills in archival preservation. She received a certificate from American University and graduate credit for completion of an intensive training course, the "Preservation and Administration of Archives," offered by the National Archives, Library of Congress and Maryland Hall of Records. The class ran from June 17 to July 12, 1957.

Throughout this period, Porter held memberships in the American Library Association (ALA), the Association for the Study of Negro Life and History (ASNLH), the District of Columbia Library Association, the Committee on Aid to African Students and other organizations. In addition, she served on the editorial board of the *Encyclopedia Africana* and the advisory panel of *Who's Who in Colored America*.

In an October 15, 1971 issue of *The Hilltop*, Howard's student newspaper, Porter reflected on her career at the Moorland Foundation, noting, "When I first started out here 41 years ago, I had to do all the typing and cataloguing myself…And about the second or third year I had 2 or 3 people working with me. But it wasn't until 10 or 12 years ago that I've had any real staff."

In her 1972–73 annual report to William Cunningham, director of University Libraries, Porter wrote that this was her forty-first and last annual report. She spoke of her plans to retire in 1973, adding, "It is my fervent desire that the collection will continue to serve the needs of scholarship."

Porter retired in June 1973, although she stayed on until September of that year, when Michael R. Winston came on board as the director of the newly organized Moorland-Spingarn Research Center (MSRC). In summing up Porter's career, Debra Newman Ham told Harriet Jackson Scarupa:

> *She became a kind of historical detective. She really learned how to sniff out or investigate leads in terms of finding out about documents and books and individuals and maintained a network of people who could help her get to materials that were historically valuable. She was a real pioneer in this effort and cared about many aspects of the historical development of Black archives and manuscript collections before other people were aware of their importance.*

Chapter 4

A MEETING PLACE FOR RESEARCHERS AT HOWARD UNIVERSITY

Speak to almost anyone who conducted research on topics in the Africana diaspora during the 1930s through the early 1970s, and they will immediately call the name of Dorothy Porter. Most researchers came to the Moorland Foundation (later Moorland-Spingarn Research Center) as part of their quest for information. While there, they were also likely to meet other researchers—lay persons, famous authors, those in the mid-level stage in their academic pursuits and students just getting started in the research process.

Many well-known and respected intellectuals and writers called on Porter's expertise, including Sterling Brown, Richard Wright, Alain Leroy Locke, Alex Haley, Langston Hughes and historians such as John Henrik Clarke, Charles Harris Wesley, Darlene Clark Hine and John Hope Franklin, as well as thousands of students, international scholars, journalists, museum exhibitors, archivists and others.

The Moorland Foundation became a popular meeting place where patrons could not only search for information on their topics but also engage in lively discussions and debates with fellow researchers. It was a haven where they could find the research materials and also research the various manuscripts of noted blacks. The letters, notes, organizational records, photographs, et cetera were the jewels that researchers looked for to make their research unique.

Porter would often invite serious scholars to her home to conduct research in her personal collection of documents accumulated over many years. She would usually give them a good meal and then duplicate materials to send to them later. Porter's home was filled with documents, especially nineteenth-century items she had acquired during her long career as a librarian, collector and researcher.

In her 1932 annual report, Porter shared an article written by an unidentified Howard student who had used the Moorland Foundation. The article, which appeared in the April 7, 1932 issue of *The Hilltop*, stated:

> *There is a pertinent element represented in the Moorland Room. Incidentally, the Moorland Room of Howard University is a unique and peculiar institution of which you should be proud. You can find works concerning Negroes and by Negroes that are available nowhere else. Personally, I have found works not available at the Library of Congress, city library, or other university libraries. The air of the place, and the competence of the Librarian in charge, will open up new vistas for you.*

Also during the late 1930s and early 1940s, to help graduate students in history and education make better use of the collections, Porter gave lectures on such topics as: "The Library and Its History," "Preparation of a Bibliography," "General Reference Books" and "Locating Materials on the Negro."

Not only did Porter go far beyond the call of duty to help students, but she also helped Howard University faculty in their research efforts as the field of black studies was coming to the forefront. Once Porter knew your topic, she would keep looking for information that would help further your research. In the 1930s, patrons working on books were even able to take out duplicate copies of materials since there were no evening hours at the Moorland Foundation.

English professor Arthur P. Davis was one of many of the Howard faculty members whom Porter helped. Located in the Dorothy Porter Wesley Papers at Yale University is an undated handwritten tribute to Porter. In this tribute, Davis wrote:

> *Dorothy Porter has made two outstanding contributions to scholars of African American literature. The first, and naturally better known, has been through her excellent bibliographical works and anthologies. The second is the personal interest she has taken in scholars coming to the Moorland-Spingarn Research Center, seeking authoritative help in their projects.*
>
> *I was the recipient of her special and invaluable attention on two occasions. When Sterling Brown, Ulysses Lee, and I were working on* The Negro Caravan, *Dorothy Porter literally turned over the resources of the*

Moorland Spingarn Center to us, giving us a key to use when the center was officially closed. She also went far beyond her routine duties in looking up not-easily-found material. Her help was crucial.

Also, when Rayford Logan wrote the history of Howard University, President Nabrit assigned me as a sort of "copyreader" for the project. Dr. Logan and I, of course, turned to Dr. Porter for help, which she gave abundantly—help that made a difference in the quality of Dr. Logan's classic work.

Historian John Hope Franklin credited Porter for the spark that ignited his forty-year project on George Washington Williams, the nineteenth-century Civil War veteran, minister, politician and historian. In 1989, Franklin reminisced to Phil McCombs in a *Washington Post* article, recalling that "I was sort of at a loss as to how to get underway. I had told Dorothy about my problems, and one day she came up to me with a letter from the Moorland-Spingarn collection, the first letter I have in my possession which Williams has written…It got me going."

Franklin further commented about Porter's help in the introduction of his book on Williams:

This key document was a letter he wrote in March 1869—when he was nineteen years old—to General Oliver Otis Howard seeking admission to that university. It was a long letter, full of misspellings and other errors to be sure, telling the general about his early life, his drifting from one town to another with his parents, his service in the army during the Civil War, and his burning desire to secure an education and be of service to this people. This letter opened up new leads to his life and his parents and siblings at his birthplace in Bedford Springs, his army career, and his training for the military.

Franklin's book *George Washington Williams: A Biography* (1985) won the 1985 Clarence L. Holte Literary Prize, which recognizes works dealing with the cultural heritage of black Americans

Another early user of the collection was E.J. Josey, a student at Howard in the 1940s. He recalled, "In spite of how busy she might have appeared or how busy she was, she was never too busy to stop and assist students. She inspired many young people, including myself, to pursue a career in librarianship." Josey thanked Porter in the preface of his 1983 book *Ethnic Collections in Libraries*. He wrote, "Dedicated to Dorothy B. Porter, the dean of ethnic collections librarians, who for more than forty years as the librarian of the Moorland-Spingarn Collection, Howard University, assembled and administered one of America's great ethnic collections."

Porter sponsored many programs to celebrate Negro History Week. The 1949 program was a poetry reading at the Moorland Foundation featuring Langston Hughes and Arna Bontemps. In a February 19, 1949 letter to Porter, Hughes wrote:

> *Certainly the highlight of my recent Negro History Week tour was my busy but delightful day in Washington and that wonderful audience which you gathered for our program. Thanks to you, too, for that enjoyable send-off which ended the evening at your house. Arna and I enjoyed it immensely, and it was a pleasure having a chance to talk quietly with old friends…Today, a very nice letter came from Mr. Reason* [Howard University librarian]. *I am glad that he was pleased with our program.*

John Bracey, chair and professor in the Department of Afro-American Studies, University of Massachusetts–Amherst, visited the Moorland Room as a child. In a May 13, 2014 e-mail to the author, he remembered:

> *I first met Dorothy Porter at some point during my years at Mott Elementary School and Banneker Junior High School* [in] *the early 1950s. Her daughter Constance was a year or two ahead of me in school. My mother, Helen Harris Bracey, taught in the* [Howard University] *School of Education and had an office on the second floor of Douglass Hall. I was allowed to go to the Moorland Room to do homework, work on Negro History projects, or read. I also used to take brief naps in that big brown leather chair—the one with the gash on the arm—that sat on the left side of the room before the entrance to the stacks. It was my favorite away-from-home study place. Mrs. Porter always was willing and eager to check on what I was reading and to help me with my assignments. When I would doubt that she actually had a real copy of a speech by Frederick Douglass, or some other figure, she would lead me into the back and take out a folder and show it to me. I wasn't allowed to touch some items because, as she informed me, even a small amount of dirt or sweat would begin the deterioration of a document. In addition to the many books and documents, Mrs. Porter showed me pictures of amazing dignified Black men and women from the nineteenth century, and made clear that if slavery did not destroy us as a people nothing in the present should be allowed to.*

Bracey further remembered Porter's continued support as he went on in the 1960s to his professional calling. He wrote:

> *During the 1960s, after I had transferred from Howard University to Roosevelt University in Chicago, I became active in the civil rights and Black Liberation movements. Every time I saw Mrs. Porter at the meetings of the Association for the Study of Negro Life and History or on a research visit, she asked how I was doing and how were my mother and sister. She always asked me to send her copies of any documents and publications of organizations I belonged to or records of activities and events I participated in. I don't know what she thought about my political views. We never talked politics as such, always history, the Association, what it was like to know Carter G. Woodson and W.E.B. Du Bois, and what wonderful new items had been added to the collections held at Moorland-Spingarn. When I began to publish books and articles, I made sure that copies were sent to Moorland-Spingarn.*

Yvonne Seon, founding director of the Bolinga Black Cultural Resources Center at Wright State University in Dayton, Ohio, met Porter in 1966 while they were both in Dakar, Senegal, attending the First World Festival of Black Arts, and they remained friends until Porter's death. In her June 21, 2014 e-mail to the author, Seon recalled:

> *I met Dorothy Porter Wesley at the first World Festival of Black and African Arts. She and Dr. [James] Porter were with the group of people that came over on the plane with a group called the American Society on African Culture. Dr. Jenkins, the president of Morgan State College, was also among those on the flight. We all stayed in a group of African-style "huts" with all the amenities that had been constructed near the airport, with a new hotel next door. A new museum of the arts had been constructed for the festival, and as I recall, Dr. [James] Porter had some works on exhibit there.*
>
> *When I got back to the States, I would often go to the Moorland-Spingarn Collection. I remember going to look up Bishop William David Chappelle after I married his grandson. She helped me locate a book he had written about his life, which included some sermons. Dorothy was passionate about seeing that the collection was used and that its treasures informed our people. She took a special interest in the people that took the collection seriously and used it. I think that was the basis for the bond between us.*

Thomas Battle told Harriet Jackson Scarupa that he did not feel warmly welcomed as a student in the 1960s. "I don't think she tolerated the casual, non-serious user very well," he said. "Her experience was in working with scholars of the first rank." In the same article, Debra Newman Ham, another Howard University History Department graduate, agreed with Battle. "You got the feeling that frivolous students couldn't use things, that you had to demonstrate the ability to get at the material."

John Rodney Clark, a 1969 graduate of Howard, remembered working as a student assistant in the Moorland Foundation. Following the seventy-fifth anniversary celebration of MSRC, Clark wrote a December 22, 1989 letter to the *Washington Post* titled "The Consummate Librarian." Clark remembered:

> *I was one of several student library aids assigned to work in the Moorland-Spingarn Collection Room…The petite woman looked up at me and exclaimed, "You have been entrusted with preserving a very important part of American culture and history." Such bold words to hear for a young college student working two part-time jobs, taking a full course load and existing during the sensational '60s at Howard University…There is an unparalleled richness in those stacks…I recall vividly her firm instructions to us on how to retrieve those rare essences of African American history and culture so that no harm would come their way…The smile, the vigor and the presence of Dr. Wesley will be forever etched in my mind and heart.*

Many authors acknowledged Porter and the Moorland Foundation staff for their assistance in helping them locate materials for their books. Among them were historians August Meier and Elliott Rudwick, who wrote many books on the African American experience. Meier complimented Porter and her staff in the acknowledgements for his 1964 book *Negro Thought in America, 1880–1915*. He wrote, "Mrs. Dorothy Porter and the staff of the Moorland-Spingarn Collection, Howard University, were particularly generous with their time and efforts in many ways."

New York University history professor William Loren Katz, in his preface to the 1974 book *Eyewitness: The Negro in American History*, wrote that Porter and her staff were among the many librarians "whose aid was essential…several went far beyond any call of duty to aid this project."

Unfortunately, not every scholar received help from Porter. In a June 25, 2014 telephone interview with the author, Elinor Des Verney Sinnette, author of *Author Alfonso Schomburg: Black Bibliophile and Collector* (1989) and retired chief librarian of MSRC, remembered that in the early 1970s, when she was working on Schomburg's biography, she asked Porter for a meeting but was refused. Porter told her, "I'm not talking to you because I'm writing my own book."

Darlene Clark Hine, Board of Trustees Professor of African American Studies at Northwestern University, wrote the following in an e-mail to the author on May 13, 2014:

> *For a long time I have thought it would be great to have individual biographies of black women librarians. We all know and appreciate the work of prominent male librarians, but few of us have the depth of appreciation for the work of Dorothy Porter in D.C. or, before her, Vivian Harsh in Chicago. This is an important project. I am pleased to share my thought about Dorothy Porter, who will always be remembered for her support and encouragement of my generation of Black women historians. I hate to think where the state of our field would be without Dorothy Porter's assistance and encouragement. Dorothy Porter was a pioneer in so many fields of intellectual endeavor. She was one of the most respected and admired African American librarians in the country. She served at Howard University for several decades and possessed incomparable knowledge of the manuscript collections that touched upon virtually every dimension of African American life and history. I was enormously grateful for her help and guidance whenever I did research at the Moorland Spingarn library, the National Archives, and the Library of Congress. She would provide suggestions as to where to look for pertinent information and often would locate helpful documents on her own that I had not requested or even knew existed. This was especially true when I was researching and writing my history of Black women in the nursing profession and later working on the study of African Americans in the medical profession. I appreciate Dorothy Porter's encyclopedic knowledge and consider her one of the absolutely essential figures who aided in the development of the field of African American Women's History. She attended the annual meetings of the Association for the Study of African American Life and History throughout her professional life. If she knew of a document, collection, or archives that would help us do exhaustive research, she would let us know. It was always a pleasure to see her, not only because she was so generous with her time and assistance but also because she was gracious, kind, and spoke the truth.*

In a June 20, 2014 e-mail to the author, Marilyn Richardson, an independent scholar and curator, related her fond memories of Porter and the wonderful advice she received as a young scholar:

One of the first things that comes to mind in remembering Dorothy is an unexpected phone call I received from her in the early 1980s. I was a fellow at the [W.E.B.] Du Bois Institute at Harvard, then headed by the late Nathan Huggins. Some of the research I was doing involved the 19th-century sculptor Edmonia Lewis. Little was known about Lewis's quite mysterious life then, and I had contacted Dorothy to ask about what she and her late husband, the pioneering African American art historian and fine artist, James Porter, had found in their search for information about her. We corresponded; she shared some documents with me and offered suggestions for possible leads to pursue.

Dorothy called one day to give me some of the best, and most succinct, professional advice I have ever received. It was in the form of a heads-up. "You are going to get a call from the Smithsonian," she told me, completely to my surprise. "They have questions for you about Edmonia Lewis. Just remember, you don't have to tell them everything you know." I cherish the wisdom, generosity, and sly protective guidance of that call from her to a younger colleague. Pure Dorothy.

A few years later, I was teaching at MIT and pursuing various projects, including a book on Maria W. Stewart, along with my Lewis research. I spent time back and forth between Cambridge, MA, and the Library of Congress, the National Archives, and the Smithsonian Museum of American Art. On one such trip, Dorothy invited me to her home to go through some Edmonia Lewis files she had there. She set me up at a small desk in a side room, and I was in researcher heaven, busily scribbling notes as she went through boxes and file cabinets retrieving folders and envelopes. At one point she even said, "Oh, you know, I believe I have some things you might want to see that are under a bed upstairs. I'll be right back."

I had to return home on an early flight the next morning, so I was eager to read through as much as I could. We agreed that I would set aside the things I'd like to have copied and sent to me. After a while, she came in to ask if I'd like to join her and her husband, Charles Wesley, for dinner. I was so immersed in my note-taking and the excitement of discovery that I thanked her but declined the invitation. I can only imagine that my parents, many hundreds of miles away, caught psychic wind of the moment and swatted me across my virtual backside, saying, "Have you lost your mind, daughter? We brought you up better than that!" Dorothy came back a few minutes later to say dinner was served and they'd welcome my company. I said I'd be honored.

Dorothy Porter with second husband, Charles H. Wesley. *JWJ MSS 93.*
Dorothy Porter Wesley Papers, James Weldon Johnson Collection in the Yale Collection
of American Literature, Beinecke Rare Book and Manuscript Library.

Ruby Sales is an independent scholar and advocate of black women's history. During 1989–90, she and the author developed an oral history program called "At Home." The program was similar to the early soirées where blacks came together in their homes to discuss topics of interest. Our "At Home" series featured black women elders. Some of the women we interviewed were Porter, librarian Jean Blackwell Hutson, poet Mae Miller

Sullivan, historian Merze Tate, nurse Elizabeth Carnegie and others. We invited people of all ages to come converse with our guests. Porter helped to identify women to invite, and she was always present and helped us ask questions from the audience of these women who were her contemporaries. In our June 29, 2014 telephone interview, Ruby remembered Porter as "a very complicated person—generous but highly critical. She shared a lot that was not in the history books. Porter was a great influence on my life and was very generous to me."

Sharon Harley, a history professor at the University of Maryland, was one of the many young scholars in Howard's History Department who benefited from working with Porter and using the resources at MSRC. Harley was considered an adopted goddaughter to Porter and Charles H. Wesley. In a May 20, 2014, telephone interview, she fondly remembered:

> [Porter] *was the consummate scholar-librarian. I worked with them at their home where they worked every day, early morning to late at night. I would get tired, and Dorothy would say, "You young people just don't have the stamina." I was impressed at how hard she worked and what primary sources meant to her. I appreciated her insight on the people she met. People like [artist] David Driscoll and [historian] John Hope Franklin were her friends. It was wonderful to be around them. They cared for young scholars and wanted to pass on their legacy to them. She was always so kind and good to us. She helped to start the spark in black women's history by writing about them and helping others get information. She cared for the Association for the Study of African American Life and History. She was just a spectacular person.*

Harley also recalled that when she got married, the reception was held at Porter's home. With a hearty laugh, Harley said, "Bernice Johnson Reagon provided the music. People forgot about my reception and started looking at all the artwork and books in their home. Porter's home was like a museum, art gallery and library all in one. Rosalyn Terborg-Penn and I dedicated our book, *Afro American Women: Struggles and Images*, to her. I saw firsthand how dedicated she was and with such high standards."

In a June 21, 2014 e-mail to the author, Yvonne Seon remembered Porter in later life as still busy publishing and enjoying her second marriage:

> *When Dr.* [James] *Porter passed, Dorothy kept herself busy with her work. It was during the period following his death that she published*

her exhaustive bibliographies of African American materials. Then one day, in her golden years, she married Dr. [Charles H.] Wesley. She was like a blushing, young bride. She admitted that she had once had a crush on him in her youth. She invited me and my mother, Beatrice Reed, to visit them at their home on North Portal Estates in D.C. Seeing her glowing in marital bliss as she entered her eighties certainly altered my impressions of the aging process! In all phases of her life, she was a vibrant and beautiful spirit.

Thomas Battle, commenting on Porter's influence on the staff said:

To MSRC staff, the patron was not just a patron. There was so much shared interest. There was always a staff member interested in the subject area of a visiting patron. Staff did not just point the patron to a book but became a part of their research. Dorothy advised the patron by sharing her own intellect and this continued on with the staff that came after her.

John Bracey has perhaps expressed best how many researchers feel about Porter's work and about her support of their projects:

Dorothy Porter, without much deserved support—financial or institutional—but with much love, insight and energy, nurtured, maintained and expanded one of the world's greatest collections of manuscripts and print materials on the African American experience. We as scholars and guardians of that experience owe Dorothy Porter a debt we can never fully repay. We owe to her memory, the obligation to try to carry on her work and legacy to the best of our abilities.

Chapter 5

DOCUMENTING THE
AFRICANA EXPERIENCE

Porter was a pioneer preservationist of Africana resources and a scholar par excellence. She not only had a passion for preserving history but was also a prolific scholar, compiling bibliographies and publishing books and articles. She was an active member of such organizations as the Association for the Study of African American Life and History, the African Studies Association and the American Antiquarian Society. She was often called on to work on special projects with these and other organizations.

Porter's expertise was known all over the world, and she was sought out by students, scholars and researchers. Her collecting and research efforts helped many to complete their own research projects, including such well-known scholars as Carter G. Woodson, John Hope Franklin, John Blassingame and Henry Louis Gates Jr., to name a few.

In 2000, Alma Dawson published an article titled "Celebrating African-American Librarians and Librarianship," which appeared in the summer issue of *Library Trends*. Dawson proclaimed:

> *Throughout their history, African American librarians have been pioneers, visionaries, risk-takers, hard workers, innovators, organizers, and achievers. Through dedication and persistence, they have developed library collections and archives in spite of limited resources. They have provided reference and information services, and their libraries have served as cultural centers for many blacks in all types of communities. Together, library educators and librarians have pioneered and persisted in achieving access to, and*

Dorothy Porter in the stacks of the Moorland Foundation, Founders Library, Howard University. *Moorland Spingarn Research Center, Manuscript Division, Howard University.*

participation in professional organizations. They have served as mentors and role models for many individuals and have contributed to the scholarly record of librarianship.

Porter was the personification of the librarian-scholar, evidenced by her untiring research and numerous publications. Writing in the May 1976 issue of the *Journal of Academic Librarianship*, Porter talked about the problems in

Dorothy Porter in the Moorland Foundation Reading Room, Founders Library, Howard University. *Moorland Spingarn Research Center, Manuscript Division, Howard University.*

acquiring Africana materials. She knew firsthand what other librarians were facing, writing:

> *With the introduction of African, Afro-American and Black Studies in American educational institutions in the late '60s and early '70s, librarians, both white and black, have been forced to examine closely their collections to discover unknown, hidden, or un-cataloged Afro-American subject matter...One of the most pressing problems librarians have faced has been the need to supply not only students but also researchers and news media with required information as quickly as possible...Serious students know that it is seldom possible to locate in one repository all materials needed for a particular research project.*

Porter became known as the expert in compiling bibliographical information on Africana history. Charles Blockson remarked:

> *She had a profound influence upon my development as a collector. We have a warm and friendly relationship. For the past forty years, collectors of African American history and literature have received a significant portion*

of their knowledge from her pioneering work in preserving black writings. The bibliographies of Dr. Porter Wesley are indispensable.

Porter often asked others to share their expertise. In an April 23, 1965 letter to poet Langston Hughes, she noted:

We are trying now to prepare for publication a bibliography of Negro authorship...I hope to have an extensive introduction well illustrated with portraits of authors and titles of books...What would we have done without Arthur Spingarn? Will you consider writing a preface for the bibliography when we are ready for this? You have been so close over the years to Arthur and to his collection that I think he would be delighted to know that you plan to do this if you consent.

Hughes responded on May 9, 1965, telling Porter, "Your bibliography sounds wonderful, and I'd be honored to do a brief intro (if I can) since I'm no authority on such."

Porter also believed that "bibliography is part of librarianship...you can't be a good librarian if you don't know the literature that you need to help scholars and students."

Porter's former co-worker Dolores Leffall, who served as both a cataloguer and reference librarian under Porter's supervision, remembered that she was "an avid bibliographer. All the librarians had to prepare bibliographies so students would know where to find resources. I worked on her published bibliographies, and was also one of the co-compilers of the series of bibliographies titled 'Current Literature on Negro Education,' published in the *Journal of Negro Education*." A Howard University publication since 1932, the aims of the *Journal of Negro Education* are to identify and define the problems that characterize the education of blacks in the United States and elsewhere, provide a forum for analysis and solutions and serve as a vehicle for sharing statistics and research on a national basis.

Porter was a supporter of other bibliographic projects and gladly wrote the foreword to the catalogue of Charles Blockson's collection at Temple University, titled *Catalogue of the Charles L. Blockson Afro-American Collection: A Unit of the Temple University Libraries* (1990). She wrote:

Charles Blockson has said that his main goal in life is to "build a good library of black history. Knowledge is a form of black power, and this is my part in it." And what an important part he has played. This monumental catalogue of the Charles L. Blockson Afro-American Collection is the result of a lifetime of dedication to the contributions that blacks have made to American society…This catalogue, among the first of its kind, is believable history. Within its pages, we learn not only the true history of a people but also what absorbing passion, industry, and patience can accomplish. With no funds except what he could find in his own pockets, Charles Blockson did what no one would have believed possible.

A few of her favorite topics for her own research were blacks in Brazil, black abolitionists, black women, David Ruggles, early African American writings, the Remond family and William Cooper Nell.

BLACK ABOLITIONISTS

Porter worked on the Yale University Black Abolitionist Papers project headed by C. Peter Ripley and George E. Carter. Ripley and Carter invited her to serve on the editorial board. According to the Black Abolitionist Papers website:

The team recognized that blacks were a pivotal and persuasive force in the nineteenth-century anti-slavery movement but that their work had been virtually ignored in scholarship prior to this collection. The team painstakingly identified black abolitionists through countless hours of research and scrutiny, bringing to light many names previously lost to history. Primary documents were gathered from more than one hundred libraries and archives across the world. The set was microfilmed and published in 1981 and quickly established a significant shift in historical scholarship regarding black leadership, activism, and community life during this period.

The digital collection reproduced in full the microfilmed content from the original collection and is now available on the Internet.

BLACK WOMEN

For those conducting research and teaching in the field of women's studies, Porter became the go-to person, especially when research materials were obscure and hard to find. Her own research on Sarah Parker Remond led the way for using innovative resources that other scholars would follow. Porter was very generous in sharing research techniques and materials.

In a January 2006 article, Jules Des Jardins wrote about her research on black librarians and the search for women's biographies. She discussed the biographical neglect of writings by and about African American women and those who addressed this problem. Des Jardins noted:

> *In the late 1940s, decades before scholars determined this dearth of written materials to be a manifestation of dissemblance, librarians at the Moorland-Spingarn Research Center at Howard and New York's Schomburg Center for Research in Black Culture helped a female researcher* [Pearl Graham] *recover the life of...Sally Hemings. Their techniques for revealing her history would run counter to all that they had come to learn as professional librarians and archivists, but their innovations teach us valuable lessons in resourcefulness that fan* [and] *benefit the craft of biography today. Their efforts to find some of the most obscure materials of race history and biography, including non-written sources, made them invaluable contributors to the New Negro history movement that took place during the years of the Harlem Renaissance.*

Porter was a strong supporter of the National Council of Negro Women (NCNW). The idea of an archives dedicated to the study of African American women's history dates back to the 1940s, when Mary Beard founded the World Center for Women's Archives. Mrs. Mary McLeod Bethune, NCNW founder, was asked to serve as one of two black sponsors of the World Center. Mrs. Bethune then asked Porter to serve as NCNW's representative on the World Center's Negro Women's Committee on Archives. After the World Center disbanded, NCNW took up the initiative to set up its own archives, and Porter served as the national chairman of this committee. NCNW achieved this milestone and, on November 11, 1979, dedicated the Mary McLeod Bethune Museum and the National Archives for Black Women's History during its First National Scholarly Research Conference on Black Women. Porter was a guest speaker at this event. Bettye Collier-Thomas served as director of the museum. The name was formally changed to the Bethune Museum and Archives, and the National Park Service named the archives as a National Historic Site in 1982. Congress passed legislation incorporating the archives into the National Park Service in 1991.

Leading twentieth-century scholars who are members of the Association of Black Women Historians (ABWH) honored Porter for her assistance in locating materials and for her pioneering scholarship. *Black Women's History at the Intersection of Knowledge and Power*, co-edited by Rosalyn Terborg-Penn and Janice Sumler-Edmond, is an anthology of twelve essays by ABWH members and honors the memory of Porter and Lorraine Anderson Williams—former chair of the Howard University History Department.

BLACKS IN BRAZIL

Looking for a publisher for her working bibliography on blacks in Brazil, Porter contacted Anthoensen Press in Portland, Maine, on January 14, 1953. In her letter, she wrote, "For many years I have noted the fine printing which has been done by your press. I have two bibliographies which I would like to have printed. One is a list of poetical works of about 700 entries. The other is a bio-bibliographical study of Brazilian works and will have about 2,500 entries." Fred Anthoensen responded on January 15, 1953, writing, "The press has printed many bibliographies and has a trained staff with years of experience, and welcomes the opportunity of doing another." He also requested a sample of the manuscripts. Nevertheless, Anthoensen Press did not publish the bibliographies.

Porter continued working on the bibliography of Brazilian materials, and in 1978, *Afro-Braziliana: A Working Bibliography* was published by G.K. Hall. This bibliography on blacks in Brazil proved to be quite popular, and on October 31, 1995, she wrote G.K. Hall about reprinting the bibliography, saying, "It would be wonderful if it were available at the 'Conference on Race, Culture and National Identity in the Afro-American Diaspora' in Gainesville, Florida, from February 21–25, 1996…this conference highlights the importance of this area of study." Porter died on December 17, 1995, and the bibliography was never reprinted.

EARLY AFRICAN AMERICAN WRITING

In a May 13, 2014 e-mail to the author, historian John Bracey related the story as told to him by Porter on how *Early Negro Writing* came about. He wrote:

> *First was Dorothy Porter's account of how she dealt with her concerns about the state of some of her beloved late eighteenth-century and early nineteenth-century materials. At some point during the late 1960s, she told me with some laughter that since white publishers were now putting everything into print they could get their hands on, she was going to get them to save some of her favorites too. In 1969, she edited a small volume* Negro Protest Pamphlets *included in the Arno Press/New York Times reprint series. Then, by her telling, she took a box of documents, pamphlets, etc. up to Beacon Press in Boston and had them published as the over 600-page volume* Early Negro Writing, 1760–1873 [1971]. *She informed Beacon Press that a second volume would be forthcoming, thus the rather arbitrary cut-off date for the first volume. For some reason,*

Dorothy Porter signing *Early Negro Writing* in California, 1988. *JWJ MSS 93. Dorothy Porter Wesley Papers, James Weldon Johnson Collection in the Yale Collection of American Literature, Beinecke Rare Book and Manuscript Library.*

that second volume never materialized. I continue to use Early Negro Writing *as a source of wisdom about our predecessors as well as a wonderful introduction to their world for my students.*

W. Paul Coates, founder of Black Classic Press, discussed in an April 17, 2014 telephone interview with the author how he came about reprinting Porter's *Early Negro Writing*:

> *It came about with me dogging her and constantly telling her that I wanted to republish something by her, anything by her. That went on for several years. She had done a number of things…*Early Negro Writing *was one of her more substantial pieces. She wanted it back out* [republished]. *Of course I was in agreement with doing it…it provided one of the earliest comprehensive looks, particularly at those writings dealing with our struggles. We got together on it. I was very concerned* [about whether] *it would appeal to her and be pleasing to her because our plan was actually to do other works. I wanted to do several of her earlier pamphlets that were out of print. As it turned out,* Early Negro Writing *was the main piece we worked on because she became ill. I remember visiting her during the time of* Early Negro Writing *to make sure everything was right, and it was always like I was in the presence of this grandmotherly queen.*

Black Classic Press did in fact republish *Early Negro Writing* shortly before Porter's death in 1995.

DAVID RUGGLES

Porter discussed David Ruggles (1810–1849) in her essay in *Black Access*. Ruggles was a book collector, abolitionist, printer and pamphleteer in the 1830s. Porter noted:

> *He maintained a circulating library of anti-slavery and anti-colonization publications and made them available to many readers at a fee of less than twenty-five cents a month. Ruggles had no time to become our first bibliophile, however, because the purpose of his book collection was to enlighten as many persons as possible to the condition in which they found themselves* [and] *to improve it as quickly as possible.*

Ruggles lived in Connecticut, New York and Massachusetts. He was an architect of the Underground Railroad and claimed to have helped more than six hundred enslaved persons escape bondage. One of the people he assisted was Frederick Douglass. Ruggles also wrote antislavery pamphlets and edited publications, including the *Genius of Freedom*, the *Colored American* and the *North Star*.

Porter published several articles about Ruggles, including a prize-winning article titled "David Ruggles, an Apostle of Human Rights," which appeared in the 1943 issue of the *Journal of Negro History*.

REMOND FAMILY

Another favorite research topic of Porter's was the Remond family of Salem, Massachusetts. Her research on the Remond family spanned the globe and took her to England, Italy and other places. Porter received a Ford Foundation grant to research the family in 1973. She also received a Prince Hall Mason Charitable Foundation grant in 1977.

Several people worked to help Porter find information on the family and opportunities to publish her research. In a March 11, 1972 letter, historian Benjamin Quarles wrote to Porter about an article she was writing on the Remonds. He advised, "The Remond article is one of the best I have read of a free black [family] in that period, not to mention the research—unusual in kind and quality. Periodicals like the *New England Quarterly* would welcome a chance to publish it."

Porter wrote biographical sketches on abolitionist and orator Charles Lenox Remond, one of which is published in the *Dictionary of American Negro Biography* (1982). She also published articles on Sarah Parker Remond. One, titled "Sarah Parker Remond: Abolitionist and Physician," appeared in the July 1935 issue of the *Journal of Negro History*. Biographical sketches were published in *Notable American Women, 1607–1950* (1971) and *Dictionary of American Negro Biography*. Additionally, Porter searched for Sarah Parker Remond's grave site for many years.

In a November 1995 interview with *Washington Post* reporter Linton Weeks, Porter said of her Remond research, "If I can just finish the book on the Remonds, I can go to heaven happy, or wherever I'm supposed to go." She died one month later.

In a June 20, 2014 e-mail to the author, Marilyn Richardson, former curator of the Boston Museum of African American History, described how, years after Porter's death, the burial place of Sarah Parker Remond was located in Italy:

> *For decades, all of the respected published sources declared that Remond had died in Rome, Italy, and was buried there in the centuries-old Non-Catholic Cemetery…There are letters in the cemetery archives from dozens of researchers, including Dorothy [Porter], asking for copies of any relevant records. Staff members found nothing to send. It was only a few years ago that two capable British historians, newly in charge of the cemetery administration, and in the process of computerizing records, solved the mystery of Remond's burial. It was known that Sarah Parker Remond had been married for a short time to an Italian man. It turns out she kept his name for the rest of her life. That, with an Italian spelling of her first name, led to her being recorded as Sara Remond Pintor.*
>
> *As is common in many old European cemeteries still in use, if there are no funds for the upkeep of a gravesite, the remains are removed after a time and reburied, respectfully, but communally. So there was no place to put a marker for Remond. Some years ago, the city of Rome, in response to such situations, agreed to allow a dozen plaques to be installed on the historic cemetery walls. I formed a committee and raised funds, and in December 2013, a plaque was placed not far from the entrance gates. It reads: "Sarah Parker Remond / Salem, MA 1824 Rome 1894 / African American Abolitionist & Physician."*

WILLIAM COOPER NELL

Porter adopted and continued the research that her second husband, Charles H. Wesley (who died in 1987), conducted for many years on William Cooper Nell (1816–1874). Nell was an abolitionist, journalist, author and civil servant in Boston.

On September 28, 1989, while a senior fellow at the W.E.B. Du Bois Institute for Afro-American Research at Harvard University (now the W.E.B. Du Bois Institute for African and African American Research), Porter discussed how she and Wesley located Nell's grave. With a Geiger stick, the specific spot was found when the sod was pulled back and plate number 1419 revealed. She persuaded the W.E.B. Du Bois Institute to put a marker on the grave of Nell at the Forest Hills Cemetery in Massachusetts and spoke at the program for the unveiling of the marker. The program and reception were held at the Boston Meeting House. The program was co-sponsored by the W.E.B. Du Bois Institute, the Boston Museum of African American History, Boston College, Boston University, Northeastern University, Roxbury Community College, Simmons College, Trotter Institute, the University of Massachusetts at Boston and Wellesley College. Randall Burkett, then associate director at the W.E.B. Du Bois Institute, said: "I well remember the cold day when we went to the cemetery to make sure it was in the right place, and I recall a small pamphlet she insisted we publish for the occasion."

The marker reads: "William Cooper Nell / Dec. 20, 1816 – May 25, 1874 / Historian / Abolitionist / Integrationist / Erected By Friends / September 1989 / 115 Years After His Death."

In an October 5, 1989 article titled "Historian's Gravesite Finally Gets Marker," written by Kay Bourne for the *Bay State Banner*, Porter is quoted as saying, "That there is a monument 'visible for all' is especially appropriate since William Lloyd Garrison, Nell's mentor and close friend, and other fellow abolitionists are all interred in this beautiful and historic place."

Porter was still working on the Nell book at the time of her death. Her daughter, Constance Porter Uzelac, completed the book. Titled *William Cooper Nell, Nineteenth-Century African American Abolitionist, Historian, Integrationist: Selected Writings, 1831–1974*, it was published in 2002 by Black Classic Press.

Porter was also an active member of many organizations, including the African Studies Association, the American Antiquarian Society, the American Library Association, the Black Caucus of the American Library Association and the Association for the Study of African American Life and History.

AFRICAN STUDIES ASSOCIATION (ASA)

Porter worked for many years with the African Studies Association (ASA). ASA is an association of scholars and professionals in the United States and Canada with an interest in the continent of Africa. Started in 1957, ASA is the leading organization of African studies in North America.

Porter joined the ASA in the 1950s and served early on as secretary and as a member of the Libraries/Archives Committee. She regularly attended the organization's conferences and committee meetings. Porter also contributed articles to the *African Studies Association Bulletin* (now the *African Studies Review*), a peer-reviewed academic journal.

In 1980, the Africana Librarians Council of the (U.S.) African Studies Association established the Conover-Porter Award. This award, given biennially, honors two pioneers in African studies bibliography: Helen F. Conover of the Library of Congress and Porter.

AMERICAN ANTIQUARIAN SOCIETY (AAS)

Porter had a long association with the American Antiquarian Society (AAS). According to the obituary by Nancy and Randall Burkett in the 1996 *Proceedings of the American Antiquarian Society*, Porter was

> *elected to membership in the society in 1970, but she had been a researcher here for years. Librarian Robert W.G. Vail opened the library for her on evenings and weekends in 1932 while she was working on her master's thesis for the Columbia University's School of Library Science so that she could complete her research in as short a time as possible. Her 1936 article entitled "Library Sources for the Study of Negro Life and History," published in the* Journal of Negro Education, *documents her high regard for AAS: "The writer, a few years ago while trying to locate imprints written by American Negroes prior to 1835, discovered that the majority of the titles found were in the American Antiquarian Society in Worcester, Massachusetts. Mr. Vail, the Librarian, does not know how many titles there are in the library on the Negro and slavery, but he writes that there are 'thousands of them.'"*

Porter came highly recommended to AAS, and the Burketts noted:

> *Roger Butterfield recommended her for membership in the Society, describing her in a letter to Marcus A. McCorison as "the leading scholar and bibliographer of Negro literature and historical materials and the organizer these days of young black librarians and bibliographers across the nation. She is a book woman in every sense—and a charming and most attractive lady." A subsequent letter from Butterfield described her as "a sparkling personality...Her election would be a great inspiration to the kind of scholarship the Society is most noted for." She was delighted with the honor of being elected a member, but was also direct in her recommendations and admonitions. When Richard Steele, Chairman of the Society's Committee on Nominations, wrote asking for names of prospective members, she*

responded: "Should you need to fill a vacancy on the Council, I would like to recommend a woman."

Porter's article "The Remonds of Salem, Massachusetts: A Nineteenth-Century Family Revisited" was published in the October 1986 *Proceedings of the American Antiquarian Society.*

AMERICAN LIBRARY ASSOCIATION (ALA) AND BLACK CAUCUS OF THE AMERICAN LIBRARY ASSOCIATION (BCALA)

Founded in 1876, the American Library Association (ALA) is the oldest and largest library association in the world. Porter became a member starting in the 1930s and attended many of the association's annual conferences. She encouraged other librarians to belong to ALA. After retirement, she remained active in ALA and was a member of its College Library Section on Non-Western Resources.

In 1970, E.J. Josey, a 1949 Howard University graduate whom Porter encouraged to be a librarian, founded the Black Caucus of the American Library Association (BCALA). BCALA serves as an advocate for the development, promotion and improvement of library services and resources to the nation's African American community and provides leadership for the recruitment and professional development of African American librarians.

Due to Porter's outstanding career as a librarian, scholar, archivist and role model for black librarians, BCALA honored her twice for her scholarship and contributions to the field. In 1972, she received the association's Distinguished Service to Librarianship Award. Porter truly met the qualifications: "Demonstrated, over a period of years, significant and continuous service to the ongoing operations, organization and growth of the Black Caucus of ALA. Exceptional progress in his/her career development that has resulted in specific and extraordinary service to the BCALA." Then, on June 24, 1990, she received BCALA's first Trailblazer Award at the association's twentieth anniversary celebration. The Trailblazer Award is the highest award given by BCALA. In honoring her, the award noted: "Porter is in a class by herself. Her achievements in the field of bibliographic studies of Black American and African history and culture has directed and influenced the entire spectrum both as a separate area of study and as an instrument for expanding the scope of mainstream academia."

Association for the Study of
African American Life and History (ASALH)

Porter had a long association with Carter G. Woodson, the "Father of Black History" and founder of the Association for the Study of Negro Life and History (ASNLH), now the Association for the Study of African American Life and History (ASALH). When she was named supervisor of the Moorland Foundation, Porter realized that she needed to learn more about Africana history. She made an appointment to visit Woodson at his home at 1538 Ninth Street NW in Washington, D.C. She joined the organization and began a relationship that would last long after Woodson's death in 1950. Both Porter and Woodson would devote their entire lives to collecting and preserving black history.

In June 1954, ASNLH gave a significant amount of materials to the Moorland Foundation. Porter documented the gift in her 1954 annual report:

> [The Moorland Foundation] *received as a gift more than 1,886 books, pamphlets, periodical issues...In addition, there were hundreds of reprints, programs, booklets, pictures, manuscripts and drawings. Several copies of essays written by Kelly Miller, the Grimké brothers and Carter G. Woodson were also included. 204 titles from French West Africa were of particular importance...There are significant foreign language publications which we would not have secured through the usual channels.*

Much of Porter's work with the ASALH is not found in written documents. Several scholars have commented on her guidance and her love for and commitment to the organization.

Karen Jefferson, former curator of manuscripts at the Moorland-Spingarn Research Center, presented a research paper on Porter at the seventy-fifth anniversary of the ASALH in 1990. Jefferson noted that Porter was a member of the ASALH Executive Council for many years and served on numerous committees. In 1948, even before she came on the council, Porter convinced Woodson to organize an advisory board to publish his *Encyclopedia Africana*. This project ended due to lack of funding.

Porter published for both the *Journal of Negro History* and the *Negro History Bulletin*, which she also indexed. She was also instrumental in persuading other librarians and faculty members at Howard to contribute articles. In addition, Porter spent a great deal of time reviewing manuscripts submitted to Woodson's publishing company, Associated Publishers.

Porter celebrated Negro History Week (now Black History Month) each year by having programs and exhibits on campus. She also helped other institutions with resources to celebrate black history.

In honoring Porter's contributions, Thomas C. Battle wrote: "Those of us who know how difficult the task is of documenting a people's history realize and appreciate the extraordinary success Dr. Porter Wesley achieved in times far more difficult than those we face today. She built the house, and we are its caretakers—we are trying our best to deserve the wonderful legacy she has left for this and future generations."

Chapter 6

LIBRARIAN/CURATOR EMERITA

After Dorothy Porter's retirement in 1973, Michael R. Winston became director of the reorganized Moorland Foundation, which had been renamed the Moorland-Spingarn Research Center (MSRC). Separate library and manuscript divisions became an integral part of the center's new program development. The new programs emphasized the identification, acquisition, preservation, research and exhibition of materials that would transform the existing special collections into a modern archival and manuscript repository and museum facility. Porter became librarian/curator emerita of the MSRC.

Several months before her retirement, Porter was the guest lecturer at the March 30, 1973 Charles Eaton Burch Lecture sponsored by Howard's English Department. Burch had been chair of the department and taught literature courses on black life and culture. Porter spoke on "The Remonds of Salem: A Forgotten Nineteenth-Century Family." Arthur P. Davis, who offered the graduate course "The Study of African American Literature," the first of its kind at the university, introduced Porter. He remarked:

> *Few, if any, persons in America today are better prepared to do the things which a collection like the Moorland-Spingarn demands. To head such a collection, the curator must be not just an administrator, but primarily a scholar-librarian. This is highly necessary in a school that emphasizes graduate work. Without a scholar-librarian to guide, advise, and suggest fields of investigation for scholars, a collection like the Moorland-Spingarn*

would lose half of its usefulness and value...Above all else, a scholar-librarian must publish. Not many scholars in her field have been as prolific as Dorothy Porter, and it is heartening to note that her productivity has not lessened with the years, as one would expect. On the contrary, it had tended to accelerate...For the last several years, Dorothy Porter has threatened to retire. This is the best example of lip service that I know. I realize that she had several flattering offers to leave Howard, but Dorothy Porter is not thinking of leaving us either through retiring or taking another position. The only thing she is going to take is her second breath, so that she can put in many more years of imaginative and dedicated service here at Howard. And we are fortunate in having her continue. We need her more than ever.

But she did retire. Yet even in retirement, Porter was as busy as ever doing what she loved—conducting research and helping others. She was also busy promoting the art and writings of her first husband, James A. Porter,

Dorothy Porter instructing Manuscript Division staff, Moorland-Spingarn Research Center, 1974. *From left to right*: Thomas Battle, Evelyn Brooks, Porter and Denise Gletten. *JWJ MSS 93. Dorothy Porter Wesley Papers, James Weldon Johnson Collection in the Yale Collection of American Literature, Beinecke Rare Book and Manuscript Library.*

Dorothy Porter's retirement reception, Founders Library, Howard University, 1973. *From left to right*: Ethel Ellis, Kenneth Wilson, Bill Cunningham, Porter and Leonie Harper. *Moorland-Spingarn Research Center, Manuscript Division, Howard University.*

Dorothy Porter's retirement reception, Founders Library, Howard University, 1973. *From left to right*: Paul Cook, Bill Cunningham, Andrew Billingsley and Porter. *Moorland-Spingarn Research Center, Manuscript Division, Howard University.*

Dorothy Porter's retirement reception, Founders Library, Howard University, 1973.
From left to right: Kenneth Wilson, Porter, Sterling Brown and Bill Cunningham.
Moorland-Spingarn Research Center, Manuscript Division, Howard University.

Dorothy Porter's retirement reception, Founders Library, Howard University, with
Marietta Harper (at podium with Porter) and MSRC staff in background, 1973.
Moorland-Spingarn Research Center, Manuscript Division, Howard University.

Dorothy Porter's retirement reception, Founders Library, Howard University, 1973. *From left to right*: Thomas Battle, Vada Butcher, Porter and Constance Uzelac *Moorland-Spingarn Research Center, Manuscript Division, Howard University.*

and working on the unfinished projects of her second husband, Charles H. Wesley. Porter loved to travel, give lectures and take part in events on the campus, especially those sponsored by the MSRC. Many honors were bestowed upon her during her retirement years.

When Howard University was notified of Porter's forthcoming retirement, it wanted to find a suitable recognition for her forty three-year career. At her retirement reception, held at the MSRC on June 8, 1973, the reading room was named the Dorothy Porter Reading Room in honor of her outstanding contributions to the Howard University and the world of scholarship.

In 1974, the MSRC published a bibliography in Porter's honor titled *Recent Notable Books: A Selected Bibliography in Honor of Dorothy Burnett Porter*. Director Michael R. Winston reported: "The Research Center staff is pleased that its first public service bibliography is dedicated to Dr. Porter, whose example as a librarian and scholar is a sturdy foundation for future development." Of Porter, Winston also commented, "Her work is continued in the newly organized Moorland-Spingarn Research Center, comprised of the Jesse E. Moorland Collection, the Arthur B. Spingarn Collection, the Howard University Museum, and the Howard University Archives."

THE C. GLENN CARRINGTON COLLECTION

C. Glenn Carrington was a bibliophile and contemporary of Porter. Over the years, the two corresponded often about their favorite topic—Africana materials. As Alain Locke's student at Howard University, Carrington had begun collecting in the 1920s. He had a passion for Alexander Pushkin, of Russian and African descent, who is considered the "Father of Russian Literature." He also collected books, manuscripts, music and many other items relating to the Harlem Renaissance.

Decades later, during the week of November 11–14, 1946, Porter visited Carrington's home in New York City to learn about the kinds of materials he collected. Porter noted in a memorandum to university librarian Joseph Reason: "The special features of the collection are his Pushkin collection and his recordings of Negro composers. Mr. Carrington gave me a few duplicate pamphlets and programs. He also promised to collect and send programs, playbills, announcements, etc. of New York concerts, lectures and meetings to us. The library needs the help and cooperation of such individuals."

After Carrington's death in 1975, Porter was instrumental in helping the MSRC acquire his collection, which had resulted from fifty years of great personal sacrifice. In size and scope, the collection was second only to the Arthur B. Spingarn Collection. And at the time of its acquisition, it was exceeded only by the Alain Leroy Locke Collection in terms of its comprehensiveness. The C. Glenn Carrington Collection contains more than 2,200 books in fifteen languages, approximately five hundred recordings and eighteen storage boxes of manuscript materials, photographs, broadsides, prints, periodicals, sheet music, newspapers and a variety of other items.

In a letter dated June 2, 1977, Winston invited Porter to participate in the installation ceremony. He wrote: "I would like to confirm the arrangements for the installation of the Glenn Carrington Collection…I am very grateful to you for agreeing to speak briefly at the installation." She accepted the invitation and gave remarks at the ceremony.

THE HOWARD UNIVERSITY MUSEUM

At the dedication of the Howard University Museum in 1979, Porter and university president James Cheek cut the ribbon to the museum. The

Dorothy Porter and Howard University president James Cheek at the dedication of the Howard University Museum, Founders Library, 1979. *JWJ MSS 93. Dorothy Porter Wesley Papers, James Weldon Johnson Collection in the Yale Collection of American Literature, Beinecke Rare Book and Manuscript Library.*

Dorothy Porter and Howard University president James Cheek at the dedication of the Howard University Museum, Founders Library, 1979. *JWJ MSS 93. Dorothy Porter Wesley Papers, James Weldon Johnson Collection in the Yale Collection of American Literature, Beinecke Rare Book and Manuscript Library.*

inaugural exhibition was titled "Toward the Preservation of a Heritage" and drew upon the resources of the Moorland-Spingarn Research Center.

The Howard University Museum was the fulfillment of Kelly Miller's dream to establish a National Negro Library and Museum. It is a teaching museum that emphasizes the visual documentation of Howard University history as well as the history of persons of African descent.

On February 12, 1979, Michael R. Winston wrote a letter expressing gratitude to Porter for participating in the dedication of the museum, stating, "I was so pleased that you could participate in the dedication of the University Museum. I had always visualized you as the person to cut the ribbon. I am delighted that circumstances permitted us to see that day come to pass."

BLACK BIBLIOPHILES AND COLLECTORS: A NATIONAL SYMPOSIUM

In her 1976 article "Bibliography and Research in Afro-American Scholarship," published in the May issue of the *Journal of Academic Librarianship*, Porter acknowledged:

> *The major centers on Afro-Americans owe their significance to a rather small circle of black bibliophiles who, for many years, knew each other and in a friendly manner aided one another to acquire rare books and pamphlets and non-print items of every kind relating to black achievements. They were all cultivated men, for the most part members of the American Negro Academy and the American Negro Historical Society. Their private libraries were often thought of as public libraries. They welcomed visitors who sought information of African and Afro-American life and history.*

Porter remarked in her essay in *Black Bibliophiles and Collectors: Preservers of Black History* (1990): "As a bibliographer, I had always wished that our antiquarian and other collectors would have compiled for us checklists of their collections with brief annotations or notes."

Porter had a special love and respect for these bibliophiles and collectors. In an April 7, 2014 telephone interview, W. Paul Coates noted:

As a group of people, the black bibliophiles were an understudied group of black activists. They were understudied by most, but Dorothy Porter knew them. She knew the bibliophiles like she knew the books they collected...She had worked with bibliophile Henry Proctor Slaughter. Part of the Slaughter Collection was here [Washington, D.C.], and part was in Atlanta (purchased in 1946). I don't know how she did all those things. When one of the great ones passed during her lifetime, she was the one called in to be there with that collection of books.

Coates further explained how the "Back Bibliophiles and Collectors" symposium came to be held at Howard University. In 1982, after he pulled together a small exhibit titled "Black Bibliophiles: Preservers of Black History" at MSRC, Karen Jefferson, senior manuscript librarian, suggested that Coates prepare a pamphlet. Working with Elinor Des Verney Sinnette, the oral history librarian and expert on bibliophile Arthur Schomburg, the decision was made to expand the exhibit and pamphlet into a national symposium. Coates recalled:

With the permission of Moorland-Spingarn director, Thomas Battle, we were able to pull together a planning grant that we took to the National Endowment for the Humanities and got the initial funding to bring people together, including Dr. Porter, to talk about how this black bibliophiles and collector's symposium would work. To have that woman, alive in the room, and to get her buy-in on something like that was fantastic...It was also necessary to have a national body of experts to endorse it so that we could at least get money to underwrite it.

The symposium was partially funded by the National Endowment for the Humanities. In the introduction to *Black Bibliophiles and Collectors: Preservers of Black History*, Thomas Battle explained: "There had previously been no comprehensive attempt to identify these dedicated individuals or to examine collectively the contributions of black bibliophiles and collectors as active forces in the struggle to preserve black history."

During the planning stages for the symposium, five black bibliophiles met with MSRC staff on March 31, 1983, to discuss their interests and careers as collectors. Along with Porter, the others in attendance were Charles Blockson of the Charles Blockson Collection at Temple University (Pennsylvania); Helen Armstead Johnson of the Helen Johnson Foundation for Theater Research (New York); James Lucas, creator of the Joys of

Heritage Collection (District of Columbia); and Ronald Rooks, appraiser, antiques dealer and publisher of the *Black Americana Collector* (Maryland). They served as the consultants and advisors to the project.

After this planning meeting and on behalf of the symposium consultants, Coates wrote Porter on April 5, 1983, expressing thanks for her participation:

> *Your anecdotes and wise counsel were the highlights of a most successful project. During the meeting, it became quite obvious that you had known all of the bibliophiles whose collections form the nucleus of some of our leading repositories. Your work as a bibliographer was central to the effectiveness of their collections as deposited in libraries and centers across the country. You have become a collector and bibliophile in your own right, although little is known and less has been written about your bibliophilic proclivities...I believe, therefore, the time has come, and indeed is past due, for your experiences and memoirs to be recorded and transcribed for posterity. To permit their loss would be an act of grave negligence on our part.*

The symposium was held in Howard University's Blackburn Center on November 29–30, 1983. Coates remarked, "It ended up being a two-day conference with an evening session...There was an evaluation process to evaluate the success of it. Part of the evaluation was that we would publish a book as a result of the conference."

Porter set the tone for the symposium by giving "The Historical Perspective," on black collectors and bibliophiles and conditions that lead to collecting. The first panel on September 29 was on "The Development of Early Private Collections." Tony Martin, professor of black studies at Wellesley College, spoke on "Bibliophiles, Activists and Race Men," and Elinor Des Verncy Sinnette spoke on bibliophile Arthur Alfonso Schomburg, for whom the New York Public Library's Schomburg Center for Research in Black Culture is named. Robert Hill of the Marcus Garvey Papers at UCLA gave the luncheon address. For the panel on "The Development of Public Collections," Jesse Carney Smith discussed the collections at Fisk University; Jean Blackwell Hutson spoke on the Schomburg Center for Research in Black Culture; Minnie Clayton discussed the collections and archives at the Atlanta University Center; and Betty Culpepper remarked on the Moorland-Spingarn Research Center. The roundtable speakers were Charles Blockson and Clarence Holte, a private collector from New York.

November 30 began with presentations on "Black Related Memorabilia as Collectibles and Material Culture." Speakers included Helen Armstead

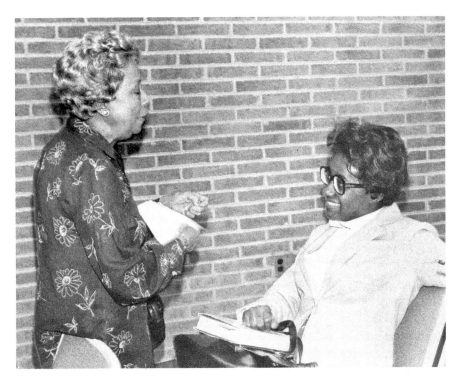

Dorothy Porter with Betty Culpepper at the Black Bibliophiles and Collectors symposium sponsored by the Moorland-Spingarn Research Center, Howard University, 1983. *JWJ MSS 93. Dorothy Porter Wesley Papers, James Weldon Johnson Collection in the Yale Collection of American Literature, Beinecke Rare Book and Manuscript Library.*

Johnson of the Johnson Foundation and Paul Robeson Jr. of the Paul Robson Archives and Image Collection. In looking at the private collectors, Valerie Sandoval Mwalilino of the Schomburg Center talked about "The Arrangements and Care of Small Book Collections," while the MSRC's Karen Jefferson spoke on "The Arrangement and Care of Manuscript Materials." Nathan Huggins of the W.E.B. Du Bois Institute at Harvard University and Bettye Collier-Thomas of the National Archives for Black Women's History spoke on "Documenting the Black Experience: Priorities for Collectors and Repositories."

The proceedings were published in 1990 by Howard University Press in a book titled *Black Bibliophiles and Collectors: Preservers of Black History.*

THE W.E.B. DU BOIS INSTITUTE FOR AFRICAN AND AFRICAN AMERICAN RESEARCH

The W.E.B. Du Bois Institute at Harvard University appointed Porter as a visiting senior scholar during the academic year 1988–89. In making the appointment, then acting director of the institute, Werner Sollars, said, "We are honored to have so distinguished a scholar at the institute this year." Porter continued her research on the Remond family and William Nell Cooper.

Randall Burkett was associate director of the W.E.B. Du Bois Institute when Porter was there. In a May 19, 2014 e-mail to the author, Burkett recalled:

> *Dorothy Porter Wesley was one of the most lively and engaging of the fellows we hosted at the W.E.B. Du Bois Institute. At 84 years of age, she was the first to arrive and the last to leave of the fellows in residence that year. She had wonderful first-hand stories about virtually all the twentieth-century individuals who were the subject of fellows' research, and she knew as much as anyone around concerning research projects dealing with the 19th century. One of my great pleasures that year was to accompany her to the Bunting Institute, the Schlesinger Library, or to the faculty club for lunch or dinner. I also loved to listen to her in conversations with longtime friends such as Adelaide Cromwell, then still teaching at Boston University. Such wonderful stories and great gossip. Those are the tidbits of history that often do not make it into the history books, and it was a pleasure to share the history "from the inside."*

On May 18, 1994, the W.E.B. Du Bois Institute announced that it had established its first endowed fund—the Dorothy Porter and Charles Harris Wesley Fund, which continues to the present day. Porter contributed to the new fund and sought to raise at least $500,000 and to name the first fellows by 1996. Income from the fund supports a yearlong residency at the institute for a doctoral candidate researching an Africana history topic. The 1994 announcement was made at a year-end party in honor of Porter. Henry Louis Gates Jr., director of the W.E.B. Du Bois Institute, told the party guests:

> *[Porter] has probably done more than any other single individual to preserve our history, to save our manuscripts, books, pamphlets and broadsides produced during our sojourn in America. Not only did she preserve the materials and make them available to countless generations of Howard University and other students and scholars; she also compiled marvelously*

valuable bibliographies...With undiminished energy, the octogenarian has at least four projects currently underway.

In the 1996 obituary of Porter that Nancy and Randall Burkett wrote for the *Proceedings of the American Antiquarian Society*, they remembered Porter at the W.E.B. Du Bois Institute:

> *She made a profound impact on that institution. She wondered, prior to the first gathering of fellows that year, how well she would fare with a group of PhD-holding colleagues. She was hardly intimidated, however, and caused general astonishment by reporting that she had the first week written "only" eighteen pages. Others were still busy unpacking boxes. Colleagues were in awe at the suggestions she offered, offhand, as each described his or her research project for the year. Her own publication record was voluminous; in addition to dozens of bibliographies and nearly one hundred articles and biographical notes, she edited valuable collections of early black writings. Her lecture on the "Remonds of Salem, Massachusetts," presented at the October 1985 meeting of the Antiquarian Society, was published in the* Proceedings *in 1986.*

THE DOROTHY PORTER WESLEY LECTURE SERIES

In April 1989, another honor was bestowed upon Porter with the creation of the Dorothy Porter Wesley Lecture Series at Howard University. The annual event was set to take place during National Library Week and was usually held during the second week in April. The series ran for twenty years from 1989 to 2008. Thomas Battle, MSRC director, said of the lecture series:

> *It was intended to provide a focus on the involvement of African Americans in the broad field of library science/library studies, as well as those who were affiliated or played important roles in the broad documentation of black history and culture. It was to reflect the broad range of activities in which she had been a participant both in history and culture as well as within the library science profession as such. She served as the lecturer in 1995, and certainly offered commentary to the various presentations, as we sought to present leading black library figures.*

Dorothy Porter speaking at the inaugural program of the Dorothy Porter Wesley Lecture Series, 1989. *Moorland-Spingarn Research Center, Manuscript Division, Howard University.*

Dorothy Porter at the inaugural program of the Dorothy Porter Wesley Lecture Series, 1989. *From left to right*: Milan Uzelac, Constance Uzelac, Porter and Karen Jefferson. *Moorland-Spingarn Research Center, Manuscript Division, Howard University.*

During the inaugural program and following the tribute from Michael R. Winston, then Howard University vice-president for Academic Affairs and former MSRC director, Porter dismissed the praise and commented with her normal quick wit, "On my 100th birthday, I want to be back to give a talk for the Dorothy Porter Wesley Lecture."

The lecture series was quite successful, with many prominent library administrators and political trailblazers coming to Howard University to honor the lady who paved the way for them to become leaders in public, national and academic institutions.

The first speaker was Robert Wedgeworth Jr., the first African American to serve as director of the American Library Association (ALA). He was president of Laubach Literacy International, publishers of basic and advanced literacy training materials.

Clara Stanton Jones, the first African American and the first woman to direct the Detroit Public Library System and also the first black president of the American Library Association (ALA), brought remarks in 1990.

E.J. Josey spoke in 1991. The title of his speech was "The Next Generation of Black Librarians." He had used the Moorland Foundation collections as a Howard University student in the 1940s.

Clara Stanton Jones speaking at the Dorothy Porter Wesley Lecture Series, 1990. *From left to right*: Karen Jefferson, Porter, Clara Stanton Jones and Elinor Des Verney Sinnette. *Moorland-Spingarn Research Center, Manuscript Division, Howard University.*

E.J. Josey speaking at the Dorothy Porter Wesley Lecture Series, 1991. *From left to right:* Thomas Battle, Porter and E.J. Josey. *Moorland-Spingarn Research Center, Manuscript Division, Howard University.*

In 1992, continuing the tradition of featuring library leaders, Jessie Carney Smith, director of the library at Fisk University and author of numerous research guides and reference books, was the guest lecturer.

Hardy Franklin, director of the District of Columbia Public Library and then president-elect of the American Library Association (ALA), spoke in 1993 on "Libraries Change Lives."

In 1994, Mary F. Lennox, dean of Library and Information Science at the University of Missouri in Columbia, spoke on "The Challenge of Information Literacy," which focused on her research on information literacy and leadership.

Although she did not live to age one hundred, Porter was the lecture speaker in 1995 at the age of ninety. That year, a special forum dedicated to

Mary F. Lennox speaking at the Dorothy Porter Wesley Lecture Series, 1994. *From left to right*: Thomas Battle, Porter and Mary F. Lennox. *Moorland-Spingarn Research Center, Archives Division, Howard University.*

her was included in the event. In handwritten notes from her presentation, "Once a Librarian, Always a Librarian," she proclaimed:

> *I don't want to talk about myself or this special library I helped create. This story has already been told…I do wish to share with you a few thoughts that have been on my mind concerning H.U. and its family…Recently my thoughts have been, "Why don't we—as librarians, historians, bibliographers, teachers and others—form a committee and research the lives and accomplishments of Howardites* [and] *write up these stories for a huge biographical* Encyclopedia Howardiana?" *As I close, let me once again urge the publication of a History of H.U. from the time Rayford Logan's 1967 book left off. Please forgive my rambling, but I hope you now feel our Howard legacy is important and should not be forgotten. Being mindful of our wonderful legacy will renew our spirit and prepare us to meet the challenges of the nineties and beyond.*

The 1995 program also included a special forum on "The Legacy of Dorothy Porter Wesley." Speakers for the forum included Thomas Battle, director of MSRC; Mohamed Mekkawi, acting director of Howard

University Libraries; Michael R. Winston, vice-president for Academic Affairs; and collector Charles Blockson. This was a day of special recognition and honor for the librarian/curator emerita.

After Porter's death in 1995, the lecture series continued in her honor. Hiram L. Davis, Library of Congress senior advisor for Staff Development and Staff Transition, gave the lecture in 1996. One of Porter's main concerns during her tenure was staff development. In his job at the Library of Congress, Davis was developing initiatives to broaden the knowledge and skills of employees.

In 1997, Representative Major Owens was the guest speaker. He was the first professional librarian to serve in the U.S. Congress. The theme for the day was "Librarians and Congress." Owens spoke on "The Political Need to Set Vital Priorities for African American Historical Research."

Augusta Alexander Clark, librarian turned Philadelphia city councilwoman, was the lecturer in 1998. As a member of the Philadelphia City Council, she focused on securing additional funds dedicated to the public schools. Clark lectured on "The Library and Local Government: An Insider Perspective."

Thomas Battle gave the 1999 lecture. Battle worked with Porter before and after her retirement. His positions at MSRC included reference librarian, curator of manuscripts and director. He spoke on "Libraries: The Adventure of Knowledge."

Jean Blackwell Hutson, a Porter contemporary and former director of the Schomburg Center for Research in Black Culture, was the guest lecturer in 2000. Her topic was "Black Librarians of the Millennium: A Century of Service." Also, a panel of Howard University librarians gave presentations on several distinguished librarians, including Virginia Lacy Jones, Augusta Baker, Virginia Proctor Powell Florence, Joseph Henry Reason, Charlemae Rollins and Edward Christopher Williams. Porter's daughter, Constance Porter Uzelac, gave a special tribute to Porter.

The 2001 lecture featured a panel of African Americans in the publishing industry. The theme was "Publishing and Selling African American Materials." George Grant, then director of the North Carolina Central University Library and president of Four-G Publishers, was the guest lecturer. The panel of speakers included author and editor D. Kamili Anderson, director of the Howard University Press; Antwan Clinton, director of the Howard University Bookstore; and W. Paul Coates, founder of the Black Classic Press.

"Toward Improved Access for All: Marketing and Libraries in the 21st Century" was the topic of Irene Owens's 2002 lecture. Owens was an associate professor in library science at the University of Texas and a former Howard University librarian. Her accomplishments include promoting the status of African Americans in the library profession and the development and implementation of resources and services for the African American community.

Stanton Biddle, a former Howard University librarian, spoke at the 2003 lecture. Biddle was national president of the Black Caucus of the American Library Association (BCALA) and a professor at the Newman Library of Baruch College. The topic of his talk was "African Americans in Librarianship."

In 2004, James C. Welbourne gave the lecture. Welbourne was the city librarian for New Haven, Connecticut's Free Public Library and was instrumental in developing literacy programs in the city. He lectured on "Separate and Unequal: Public Libraries in Black Communities from Plessy to Brown."

Howard graduate Beacher Wiggins spoke at the 2005 lecture. A career librarian at the Library of Congress, Wiggins was acting associate librarian for Library Services and director of the Acquisitions and Bibliographic Control directorate. As such, Wiggins made valuable contributions to the international cataloguing mission of the Library of Congress.

Andrew P. Jackson (aka Sekou Molefi Baako), known as an "activist librarian," gave the 2006 lecture. He was the executive director of the Langston Hughes Community Library and Culture Center in Queens, New York City, and executive director of the Black Caucus of the American Library Association (BCALA). Baako promoted the use of libraries for empowerment just as Porter did.

Charles Blockson was the guest speaker for the 2007 lecture. He discussed "The Making of Legacy: Treasures of Black History."

The 2008 lecture was the last lecture in the series. It was also the twentieth anniversary for the series, and the theme was "Celebrating 20 Years." Elinor Des Verney Sinnette, retired MSRC chief librarian, and Mohamed Mekkawi, Howard University library director, were the guest speakers.

The lecture series was a fitting tribute to Porter, a woman who knew and worked with many of the speakers and also helped many of them in their quest to make library services available to all citizens.

In an April 28, 2014 interview, Thomas Battle remarked, "No speaker came who did not talk about Porter and the influence she had on their life's work. It was also important to honor her to a newer audience of folk who could benefit from her wisdom."

THE SEVENTY-FIFTH ANNIVERSARY OF THE MOORLAND-SPINGARN RESEARCH CENTER

December 18, 1989, marked the seventy-fifth anniversary of the Moorland-Spingarn Research Center. Porter was among those honored at the gala reception held on December 16 in the Blackburn Center.

Speaking at the celebration, historian John Hope Franklin said of MSRC, "Certainly for forty-five-plus years I've been in and out of this collection. I was present at Howard when Arthur Spingarn presented this collection [in 1946] that made it the Moorland-Spingarn collection."

Thomas Battle commented on the forty-five dedicated MSRC staff to Phil McCombs, who covered the event for the *Washington Post*, "[They] could probably make a good deal more money working elsewhere but stay because of their love and devotion for the subject."

THE CENTENNIAL CELEBRATION OF MORDECAI W. JOHNSON'S BIRTH

On January 12, 1990, MSRC sponsored a symposium celebrating the 100th birthday of Mordecai W. Johnson, Howard University president from 1926 to 1960. The theme for the event was "Mordecai Wyatt Johnson: The Man and His Times." Clifford Muse, university archivist, served as moderator for the program. For the morning session held in Rankin Chapel, interim president Carlton Alexis gave a statement on behalf of the Howard community. A panel discussion titled "Scholarly Reflections [on Johnson]" was also held. Panelists included Carroll L. Miller, dean of the Graduate School, and Vincent J. Browne, political science professor, representing Howard University. The visiting scholars on the panel were Herman R. Branson, president emeritus of Lincoln University, and Stephen J. Wright, commissioner with the Virginia State Council on Higher Education.

Michael R. Winston, vice-president for Academic Affairs, gave the afternoon statement on behalf of the Howard community. The afternoon session was held in the Blackburn Center with a panel titled "Howard Reminiscences" and included Johnson's daughter, Carolyn Johnson Graves; history professors Harold Lewis and Martha Putney; and Dorothy Porter, librarian/curator emerita of MSRC. Panelists shared personal memories of

Symposium celebrating the centennial birthday of Mordecai W. Johnson, the first African American president of Howard University, who served from 1926 to 1960. *From left to right*: Porter, Martha Putney, Harold Lewis and Carolyn Johnson Graves, 1990. *JWJ MSS 93. Dorothy Porter Wesley Papers, James Weldon Johnson Collection in the Yale Collection of American Literature, Beinecke Rare Book and Manuscript Library.*

the man who became Howard University's eleventh and first black president and who led the university for thirty-four years.

THE LIBRARY OF CONGRESS AFRICAN AMERICAN MOSAIC SYMPOSIUM

Upon the publication of *The African American Mosaic: A Library of Congress Resource Guide for the Study of Black History and Culture* (edited by Debra Newman Ham), a symposium was held on February 23, 1994. This was the first guide to the library's extensive collections of African American materials. Many scholars, researchers, writers and others gathered to discuss this groundbreaking resource that accompanied the exhibit by the same name and is still available online.

Porter was among the speakers on the panel titled "The Library's Collections and Historical Research." She discussed how she used the Library of Congress for her research projects. After expressing her delight in getting an advanced copy of *The African American Mosaic*, she noted that she planned to finish two more books and that the citations in the guide would save her valuable time and energy in using the collections. Porter also discussed her seventy-year association with the Library of Congress as she worked on such bibliographies as *North American Negro Poets: A Bibliographical Checklist of Their Writings, 1760–1944* (1945). She said that this project required her to walk the library's stacks, examining each book for title page notations such as "by a person of color" or "by an African." Porter called *The African American Mosaic* "a whole history…of my people."

THE NATIONAL ENDOWMENT FOR THE HUMANITIES CHARLES FRANKEL PRIZE

In 1988, the National Endowment for the Humanities (NEH) established the Charles Frankel Prize to recognize persons for outstanding contributions to the public's understanding of the humanities. Frankel was an American

President Bill Clinton, Porter and Constance Uzelac in the Grand Foyer of the White House during the reception for the NEH Charles Frankel Prize, October 14, 1994. *JWJ MSS 93. Dorothy Porter Wesley Papers, James Weldon Johnson Collection in the Yale Collection of American Literature, Beinecke Rare Book and Manuscript Library.*

philosopher, assistant U.S. Secretary of State, professor and founding director of the National Humanities Center.

In 1994, Porter was one of five individuals to receive the prize. Her citation read: "Librarian whose pioneering work as an archivist of African-Americana helped lay the foundation of African-American studies programs." The prize was presented at the White House by President Bill Clinton on October 14, 1994.

Dorothy Porter Wesley was truly a librarian/curator emerita. She often came back to assist staff and to attend public programs. She also continued her own research and writing with an intellect and curiosity that remained strong even into her nineties.

Chapter 7

THE DOROTHY PORTER WESLEY COLLECTIONS

orter stated in the paper that she delivered at the 1983 Black Bibliophiles and Collectors symposium, "I do not call myself a collector." However, the then seventy-eight-year-old Porter was indeed a collector and had been for more than fifty years, filling her five-bedroom home to the brim with books, pamphlets, prints and other artifacts of historical significance. She also saved the collections, papers, letters and manuscripts of her first husband, James Amos Porter, an artist, a pioneer in the field of African American art history and head of the Howard University Department of Art, where he taught for more than forty years; and her second husband, Charles Harris Wesley, a historian who wrote more than twenty books, an ordained minister in the African Methodist Episcopal Church, a former dean of the Howard University College of Liberal Arts and Graduate School and former president of both Wilberforce University and Central State College. Wesley also served as the historian of his fraternity, Alpha Phi Alpha, for more than seventy years. Porter would continue to accumulate books and other items until her death on December 17, 1995.

Constance "Coni" Porter Uzelac, Porter's only child (who had no children) moved Porter from Washington, D.C., to her home in Fort Lauderdale, Florida, where they filled Uzelac's home and a two-bedroom apartment with the collections of Charles Wesley, James Porter and Dorothy Porter Wesley. Upon her mother's death, Uzelac inherited all three collections.

Uzelac, a medical librarian who received her bachelor's degree from Howard University and her master's degree from the Catholic University of America

Dorothy Porter and daughter Constance Uzelac enjoying Porter playing the organ, 1980.
JWJ MSS 93. Dorothy Porter Wesley Papers, James Weldon Johnson Collection in the Yale Collection of American Literature, Beinecke Rare Book and Manuscript Library.

Department of Library and Information Science, became the full-time curator of the collections and expressed an interest early on in selling them.

In an August 25, 1999 article by Audra Burch in the *Miami Herald*, Uzelac commented: "Ideally, I would like to keep the collections together and place it where its value will be recognized and there is a budget available to allow it to grow." Burch reported that a curator at the Library of Congress took a look at portions of the collection in 1996 and that the library remained interested in acquiring it, as did the Smithsonian Institution. Fleur Paysour, director of public affairs at the Smithsonian's Anacostia Museum, said: "Yes, we would love to have the [Uzelac] collection. What she has is very important and worthy of being collected, put in one place, preserved, exhibited from time to time, put on tour and archived in a way that curator[s] and researchers could have access to it."

Between 1996 and 1999, Uzelac established the Dorothy Porter Wesley Research Center, Inc. in Fort Lauderdale, Florida, in a storefront on Las Olas Boulevard. In August 1999, as plans were made for the groundbreaking of the Broward County Library African-American Research Library and Cultural Center (AARLCC), Uzelac wrote a letter to Samuel F. Morrison, director of the library and founder of the AARLCC, that vividly describes the three collections that she collectively calls the Dorothy Porter Wesley Archives:

> *The Archives contains printed material including books (fiction and non-fiction) periodicals, journals and serials, newspapers and newsclippings [sic], scrapbooks of newsclippings, broadsides, pamphlets and brochures, sheet music and cookbooks.*
>
> *The non-print material include a large doll collection, figurines, bottles, commemorative plates and silverware, handwritten documents, numerous unpublished papers, diaries and notebooks, lectures and speeches, pottery, photographs, correspondence, book drafts, at least two dozen unusual bookends (!) maps, prints, and other visual materials such as postcards, memorabilia, postcards [sic] and stamps, phonographic recordings and tapes (audio and video)...*
>
> *At this point, I will only illuminate that the contents of the collection of James Amos Porter...includes works (oil, drawings, pastels, watercolors, prints and lithographs) by Charles White, Elizabeth Catlett, David Driskell, Mildred Thompson, Lloyd McNeil, Charles McGee, Hughie Lee-Smith, Lois Mailou Jones, Alice Gafford, Camille Billops, Charles Sallee...and others. There is sculpture, metalwork, pottery, drawings, prints, lithographs, signed posters and a large slide collection, including 800 or so taken in West Africa, Egypt and Brazil.*
>
> *The papers of Charles Harris Wesley are an eclectic collection of documents, pamphlets, early historical writings, photocopied manuscripts, correspondence, and much more...*

Uzelac also notes that her first priority was to produce a checklist of the five thousand to six thousand books, monographs, pamphlets and other printed materials. In addition, she suggested pay for her services as a consultant with the AARLCC assigned to work on the Dorothy Porter Wesley Collection.

In July 2000, Jane S. Knowles, acting director of the Schlesinger Library at Harvard University's Radcliffe Institute for Advanced Study, and Susan Von Salis, an archivist at the library, visited Uzelac to survey the Dorothy Porter Wesley Collection. Knowles wrote a letter to Uzelac dated July 11, 2000, in which she states:

> *We are now exploring with the Du Bois Institute how to acquire the whole collection for Harvard...You have said all along how important it is to keep everything together. We agree. It would be hard to separate anything: each section of the collection interconnects with the others...most important to us*

Camille Billops and Dorothy Porter at the Hatch-Billops Collection, New York, May 20, 1990. *JWJ MSS 93. Dorothy Porter Wesley Papers, James Weldon Johnson Collection in the Yale Collection of American Literature, Beinecke Rare Book and Manuscript Library.*

is the historical value of the papers...of paramount interest is her [Dorothy Porter's] *work as a scholar librarian, her correspondence with other collectors, and the files that show how she built one of the principal African American libraries. Your father's correspondence, art files, catalogues, and research files illuminate the life of a scholar, artist, and are important for the study of African America Art, the art of the Caribbean, and of Africa. Charles Wesley's papers offer opportunities for the study of a most distinguished Harvard educated historian, university president and eminent historian.*

And in a letter dated December 11, 2000, Knowles wrote:

We have a donor who is prepared to offer on our behalf a substantial portion of your asking price but only if we can purchase all the family papers (DPW, CAW [CHW], *JAP). We would exclude from the materials to be purchased: all books and periodicals; all art work; and all the rare items that you designated 3rd party Afro and non-Afro correspondence...We would therefore like to extend an offer of $300,000 for the DPW, CAW* [CHW], *JAP family papers...In sum, the sale would include the 215 cartons and 147 file boxes surveyed by Susan and me in July...Our donor*

*is unfortunately unable to enter into prolonged negotiations and we suggest
that if you are interested in our offer, we conclude the sale and transfer of
materials by the end of March.*

The sale and transfer of the papers to the Schlesinger Library did not happen.

The AARLCC opened in October 2002, and in October 2003, it purchased fifty-three boxes of materials containing 5,200 items (primarily books and pamphlets) from Uzelac to form the Dorothy Porter Wesley Collection, 1852–1995. According to the "Collection Overview," the primary material is from the years 1930–85 and includes "printed materials, correspondence, writings and photographs primarily focusing on African American history and culture; a small portion of the collection focuses on Afro-Brazilian and Brazilian culture. A substantial part of the collection is made up of photocopies and reproductions of title pages…Within the collection, the pamphlet files contain the largest number of original prints." The amount that AARLCC paid for the collection is not available to the public.

In 2009, Uzelac put all three collections up for auction separately with the Swann Auction Galleries. The James Amos Porter Collection was sold on February 25, 2010, for $50,400 to Emory University. The Charles Harris Wesley Collection was sold on March 10, 2011, for $43,200 to Alpha Phi Alpha Fraternity. And the Dorothy Porter Wesley Collection was sold to Yale University's Beinecke Rare Book and Manuscript Library via the William Reese Company for $43,200 on March 1, 2012, less than eight weeks before Uzelac died on April 23, 2012, after a long battle with cancer.

The Dorothy Porter Wesley Papers are part of the James Weldon Johnson Collection in the Yale Collection of American Literature. The "Provenance" statement in the "Guide to the Dorothy Porter Wesley Papers" notes that the collection came to the Beinecke Library in three installments in 2012. Materials housed in boxes 1–72 were received directly from Swann Auction Galleries. The materials housed in boxes 73–116 were received in July from the William Reese Company after shipment from Florida, where they were found in storage "by Wesley's family." And in November, materials housed in boxes 112–126 were received via the William Reese Company after "Wesley's family" sent additional materials to the Swann Auction Galleries. The unprocessed collection is available for public use.

The Beinecke Library's summary of the Dorothy Porter Wesley Collection notes: "The collection consists chiefly of the correspondence, writings, biographical materials, research files, photographs, and personal papers of Dorothy Porter Wesley. The bulk of the collection is comprised of research materials relating to various subjects relating to African American history, culture, and bibliography…"

Yale University senior Julie Botnick used the Dorothy Porter Wesley Collection to write a paper titled "'I Am Sure That You Know Yourself That It Is a Very Good Job': The Early Life and Library of Dorothy Porter" for her "Art of Biography" class. She writes:

> *The archive of Dorothy Porter Wesley is a collection of ephemeral memories. At one point, she started keeping everything, even her troubled sister Alice's recipe collection… The papers of the woman who, in her life, was so meticulous about collecting and cataloging are barely processed… There is a pack of flossers in Box 97, likely signifying that someone literally swept Porter's entire office into boxes indiscriminately before shipping.*

The papers of James Porter at Emory University are also unprocessed and available to the public. They are housed in fifty-three boxes. The "Descriptive Summary" states that the collection consists "primarily of research and correspondence files related to the publication of Modern Negro Art and his tenure at Howard University."

The papers of Charles Wesley are unprocessed and not yet available to the public. The description from the Swann Auction Galleries Catalogue notes that the collection "consists of over 30 boxes, three of them containing an Autobiography, with supporting material and correspondence (up to and including 1965); six boxes of general correspondence arranged chronologically, three boxes devoted to the Alpha Phi Alpha Fraternity, two boxes of material relating to the Association for the Study of African-American Life and History… several boxes relating to Central State and Wilberforce…and much more."

THE LEGACY OF DOROTHY PORTER WESLEY

Dorothy Porter Wesley, the doyenne of Africana bibliography, built a premier collection of resources by and about persons of African descent at Howard University. During her forty-three-year tenure, she added thousands of books, pamphlets, serials, manuscripts, photographs, sheet music and ephemeral materials to what would become the Moorland-Spingarn Research Center. As future scholars, researchers, librarians and archivists continue building on her work and documenting this rich heritage, her legacy <u>will</u> live on.

AFTERWORD

G reat institutions exist because extraordinary people commit themselves to making them great. Howard University's Moorland-Spingarn Research Center will celebrate the centennial of its founding in December 2014. Known first as the Moorland Foundation in honor of Howard University alumnus and trustee Jesse Moorland, it was renamed the Moorland-Spingarn Research Center in 1973 in honor of the two bibliophiles whose collections on the black experience were the most distinguished ones held by the center at that time. The Arthur Spingarn Collection, a unique collection of some five thousand books by authors of African descent from Africa, the Caribbean and Latin America, as well as the United States, was one of the most distinguished collections on the black experience in private hands when Dorothy Burnett Porter (Wesley) convinced Howard University to acquire it in 1946. When added to Jesse Moorland's and other smaller Africana collections at Howard, it made the Moorland Foundation and its successor, the Moorland-Spingarn Research Center, the leading research library on the black experience in an academic university setting.

We should not be surprised that the Moorland-Spingarn Research Center is named for these great bibliophiles. The Schomburg Center, like the Slaughter Collection at Atlanta University and the Charles Wright Museum in Detroit, is named for an individual who amassed its founding and foundational collections. In at least two instances, however, two extraordinary women who committed themselves to making their respective institutions great deserve at least equal recognition. I am referring to Dorothy Burnett Porter (Wesley) and Jean Blackwell Hutson. The two shared similar histories. Both were graduates of the Columbia University

School of Library Service. Porter was the first African American graduate in 1932 and Jean Hutson the second in 1936. Both worked for a period of time at the Schomburg Collection in Harlem before being selected to lead their respective institutions. Hutson was not named to head the Schomburg Collection until 1946, but for thirty-six years, she devoted her life to building and providing access to that center's holdings.

Dorothy Porter (Wesley) did the same for the Moorland Foundation and its successor. By the time she retired in 1973, she had increased the Moorland's holdings from its namesake's 6,000 items and Arthur Spingarn's 5,000 items to over 150,000 volumes of books, plus newspapers, microfilm, serials and manuscript and archival records. Her service to scholars; to the fields of African American, African and African Diaspora scholarship; and to the preservation of black history and culture in the United States and Africa is legendary. This book is a commendable introduction to her extraordinary life and times. We eagerly await the fuller biography Dr. Sims-Wood so urgently recommends.

CODA

In 1972, I was interviewed as a candidate to succeed Dorothy Porter in her role at the Moorland Foundation. I was in the third year of my doctoral program at the University of California–Berkeley. I was uncertain about whether I wanted to continue my studies there, and I was asked by the then-director of the Howard University Libraries to interview for the position Porter was vacating. I felt, however, that I was not ready for the challenge, and I believed the university had a much stronger candidate in Dr. Michael R. Winston, who had recently graduated from Berkeley's history department.

I went back to Berkeley, finished my course work, advanced to candidacy and started working professionally at Atlanta's Institute of the Black World. Almost forty years later, after twenty-seven years of building on the legacy of Jean Blackwell Hutson's Schomburg Center, I was asked to direct the Moorland-Spingarn Research Center. I am ready now, and I am committed to continuing to develop the Moorland-Spingarn Research Center, including celebrating and promoting the legacy of Dorothy Porter Wesley.

HOWARD DODSON
Director
Moorland-Spingarn Research Center
Howard University

Appendix A

AWARDS AND ACCOLADES RECEIVED BY DOROTHY PORTER WESLEY

Without exaggeration, there hasn't been a major black history book in the last 30 years in which the author hasn't acknowledged Mrs. Porter.
—*Benjamin Quarles, 1973*

Julius Rosenwald Scholarship for study toward master's degree (1931–32)

Julius Rosenwald Fellowship for research in Latin American literature (1944–45)

Ford Foundation Fellowship to fund acquisitions and work onsite at the National Library of Nigeria in Lagos (1962–64)

American Studies Association travel grant for travel to Accra, Ghana, to attend the First International Congress of Africanists (1962)

D.C. Chapter of the National Barristers Wives for outstanding service in the area of human relations (August 2, 1968)

Honorary Doctor of Letters, Susquehanna University, Selinsgrove, Pennsylvania (June 1971)

Black Caucus of the American Library Association—Distinguished Service Award (1972)

Howard University Institute for the Arts and the Humanities, First Annual Symposium on Creative Expression dedicated to Porter and Arthur P. Davis (April 10, 1973)

Dedication of the Dorothy B. Porter Room in Founders Library, Howard University (June 8, 1973)

Ford Foundation grant for research on the Remond family (1973)

Dorothy Porter receiving the Howard University Alumni Award, 1974. *JWJ MSS 93.*
Dorothy Porter Wesley Papers, James Weldon Johnson Collection in the Yale Collection of American Literature, Beinecke Rare Book and Manuscript Library.

Howard University Alumni Award for Distinguished Achievement (March 1, 1974)

Certificate of membership in the Howard University 500 Club (July 1975)

Delta Sigma Theta Sorority Bicentennial Award (August 11, 1976)

U.S. Department of the Interior Heritage Conservation and Recreation Services for contribution to the preservation of America's cultural resources (November 19, 1976)

Prince Hall Masons Charitable Foundation grant for research on the Remond family (1977)

Conover-Porter Award established by the Africana Librarians Council of the African Studies Association (US) named in honor of Porter and Helen F. Conover and is presented biennially (1980 – present)

Martin Luther King Jr. Leadership Award presented by the District of Columbia Public Library at the Martin Luther King Jr. Memorial Library on the twentieth anniversary of the March on Washington (August 28, 1983)

Pennsylvania Historical and Museum Commission issued a set of resolutions honoring Porter's achievements (April 3, 1985)

Schomburg Center for Research in Black Culture included a photograph of Porter in an exhibition of "Fifteen Great Afro-Americans of the Century" (1986)

Included in Carl Van Vechten collection of photogravures made from original negatives in "'O', Write My Name" exhibit, curated by Schomburg Center for Research in Black Culture, Traveling Exhibit, (1986–present)

Visiting Senior Scholar, W.E.B. Du Bois Institute for Afro-American Research at Harvard University (1988–89)

The Library Company of Philadelphia presented a silver plaque in honor of achievements (April 15, 1989)

Honorary Doctor of Humane Letters, Syracuse University, Syracuse, New York (May 1989)

Annual Dorothy Porter Wesley Lecture at the Moorland Spingarn Research Center, Howard University (1989–2008)

Olaudah Equiano Award for Excellence for Pioneering Achievements in African-American Culture, Ethnic Studies Program, University of Utah, Salt Lake City, Utah (October 27, 1989)

The Black Caucus of the American Library Association first Trailblazer Award (June 24, 1990)

Honorary Doctor of Humane Letters, Radcliffe College, Cambridge, Massachusetts (February 23, 1990)

National Caucus and Center on Black Aged Living Legacy Award (November 15, 1992)

Ceremonial Resolution by the Council of the District of Columbia honoring Porter's achievements (1993)

Award for Distinguished Service in Documentary Preservation and Publication (November 4, 1993)

Women of All Colors honored the life and contributions of Porter at the opening of the Women of All Colors National Headquarters and the Rep Theatre Company Inc.'s 1993–94 season (December 12, 1993)

National Endowment for the Humanities Charles Frankel Prize presented by President Bill Clinton at the White House (October 14, 1994)

Certificate of Recognition from the Alpha Wives of Washington, D.C., on the occasion of the installation of their archives at the Moorland-Spingarn Research Center, Howard University (June 10, 1994)

The Office for the Advancement of Public Black Colleges, the National Association for Equal Opportunity in Higher Education and the College Fund Lifetime Achievement Award (posthumous, February 1996)

Dorothy Porter Wesley Life Achievement Recognition Resolution of 1996 issued by the District of Columbia Council (posthumous, 1996)

Appendix B

A SELECTED BIBLIOGRAPHY

OF PUBLICATIONS BY

DOROTHY PORTER WESLEY

BOOKS AND MONOGRAPHS

Porter, Dorothy B. *Afro-Braziliana: A Working Bibliography*. Boston: G.K. Hall, 1978.

————. *Early Negro Writing, 1760–1837*. Boston: Beacon Press, 1971. Reprint, Baltimore, MD: Black Classic Press, 1995.

————. *North American Negro Poets: A Bibliographical Checklist of Their Writings, 1760–1944*. Hattiesburg, MS: Book Farm, 1945.

————, comp. *Howard University Masters' Thesis Submitted in Partial Fulfillment of the Requirements for a Master's Degree at Howard University, 1918–1945*. Washington, D.C.: Howard University Graduate School, 1946.

————, comp. *The Negro in American Cities: A Selected Annotated Bibliography*. Washington, D.C.: Howard University Library, 1967.

————, comp. *Working Bibliography on the Negro in the United States*. Ann Arbor, MI: Xerox, University Microfilms, 1969.

————, ed. *A Catalogue of the African Collection in the Moorland Foundation, Howard University Library*. Washington, D.C.: Howard University Press, 1958.

————, ed. *Negro Protest Pamphlets: A Compendium*. New York: Arno Press, 1969.

Porter, Dorothy B., and Ethel M. Ellis, comp. *Journal of Negro Education: Index to Volumes 1–31, 1932–1962*. Washington, D.C.: Howard University Press, 1963.

BIOGRAPHICAL SKETCHES

Porter, Dorothy B. "Charles Lenox Remond." In *Dictionary of American Negro Biography*, edited by Rayford W. Logan and Michael R. Winston. New York: W.W. Norton, 1982. 520–22.

———. "Daniel Jackson Sanders." In *Dictionary of American Biography*, edited by Dumas Malone. New York: Charles Scribner's Sons, 1935. 8:332.

———. "David Ruggles." In *Dictionary of American Negro Biography*, edited by Rayford W. Logan and Michael R. Winston. New York: W.W. Norton, 1982. 536–38.

———. "Edward Christopher Williams." In *Dictionary of American Negro Biography*, edited by Rayford W. Logan and Michael R. Winston. New York: W.W. Norton, 1982. 655–56.

———. "Harriet Tubman." In *Dictionary of American Biography*, edited by Dumas Malone. New York: Charles Scribner's Sons, 1936. 10:27.

———. "Henry Proctor Slaughter." In *Dictionary of American Negro Biography*, edited by Rayford W. Logan and Michael R. Winston. New York: W.W. Norton, 1982. 558–59.

———. "Joshua Brown Smith." In *Dictionary of American Negro Biography*, edited by Rayford W. Logan and Michael R. Winston. New York: W.W. Norton, 1982. 565–66.

———. "Maria Louise Baldwin." In *Dictionary of American Negro Biography*, edited by Rayford W. Logan and Michael R. Winston. New York: W.W. Norton, 1982. 21–22.

———. "Mary Edmonia Lewis." In *Dictionary of American Negro Biography*, edited by Rayford W. Logan and Michael R. Winston. New York: W.W. Norton, 1982. 393–95.

———. "Monroe Nathan Work." In *Dictionary of American Negro Biography*, edited by Rayford W. Logan and Michael R. Winston. New York: W.W. Norton, 1982. 667–68.

———. "Patrick Henry Reason." In *Dictionary of American Negro Biography*, edited by Rayford W. Logan and Michael R. Winston. New York: W.W. Norton, 1982. 517–19.

———. "Pauline E. Hopkins." In *Dictionary of American Negro Biography*, edited by Rayford W. Logan and Michael R. Winston. New York: W.W. Norton, 1982. 325–26.

———. "Sarah Parker Remond." In *Dictionary of American Negro Biography*, edited by Rayford W. Logan and Michael R. Winston. New York: W.W. Norton, 1982. 522–23.

BOOK CHAPTERS

Porter, Dorothy B. "Africana at Howard University." In *Handbook of American Resources for African Studies*, edited by Peter Duignon. Stanford, CA: Stanford University, Hoover Institution on War, Revolution and Peace, 1967. 33–39.

———. "A Bibliographical Checklist of American Negro Writers about Africa." In *Africa Seen by American Negroes*. Paris: Présence Africaine, 1958. 79–99.

———. "Fifty Years of Collecting." In *Black Access: A Bibliography of Afro-American Bibliographies*, compiled by Richard Newman. Westport, CT: Greenwood Press, 1984. xvii–xxviii.

———. "The Librarian and the Scholar: A Working Partnership." In *Proceedings of the Institute on Materials by and About the American Negro*. Atlanta, GA: Atlanta University School of Librarianship, 1967. 71–80.

———. "The Water Cure—David Ruggles." In *The Northampton Book: Chapters from 300 Years in the Life of a New England Town, 1654–1954*. Northampton: Northampton, Massachusetts Tercentenary History Committee, 1954. 121–26.

Wesley, Dorothy Porter. "Black Antiquarians and Bibliophiles Revisited, with a Glance at Today's Lovers of Books and Memorabilia." In *Black Bibliophiles and Collectors: Preservers of Black History*, edited by Elinor Des Verney Sinnette, W. Paul Coates and Thomas C. Battle. Washington, D.C.: Howard University Press, 1990. 3–20.

ARTICLES

Porter, Dorothy B. "African and Caribbean Creative Writing: A Bibliographic Survey." *African Forum* 1 (Spring 1966): 107–11.

———. "The Anti-Slavery Movement in Northampton." *Negro History Bulletin* 24 (November 1960): 33–34, 41.

———. "Bibliography and Research in African-American Scholarship." *Journal of Academic Librarianship* 2 (May 1976): 77–81.

———. "The Black Role During the Era of the Revolution: A Little Known Chapter of Afro-American History Is the Subject of a Show at the Smithsonian's National Portrait Gallery." *Smithsonian* 4 (August 1973): 52–57.

———. "Books with Negro Characters for Children." *National Educational Outlook Among Negroes* 1 (December 1937): 33–36.

———. "Early Manuscript Letters Written by Negroes." *Journal of Negro History* 24 (April 1939): 199–210.

———. "Family Records: A Major Resource for Documenting the Black Experience in New England." *Old Time New England* 63 (Winter 1973): 69–72.

———. "Fiction by African Authors: A Preliminary Checklist." *African Studies Bulletin* 5 (May 1962): 54–60.

———. "Library Resources for the Study of Negro Life and History." *Journal of Negro Education* 5 (April 1936): 232–44.

———. "The Organized Educational Activities of Negro Literary Societies, 1828–1846." *Journal of Negro Education* 5 (October 1936): 555–76.

———. "Research Centers and Sources for the Study of African History." *Journal of Human Relations* 8 (1960): 54–63.

BOOK REVIEWS

Porter, Dorothy B. "An American Heroine." Review of *Harriet Tubman* by Earl Conrad. *Journal of Negro Education* 13 (Winter 1944): 91–93.

———. "Drum, A South African Periodical." Review of *Drum: The Newspaper That Won the Heart of Africa* by Anthony Sampson. *Journal of Negro Education* 27 (Spring 1958): 164–66.

———. "Fiction by Negro Authors." Review of *A Century of Fiction by American Negroes, 1853–1952* by Maxwell Whiteman. *Journal of Negro Education* 25 (Spring 1956): 146.

———. "A Guide to the National Capital." Review of *Washington, City and Capital* by the Works Progress Administration. *Journal of Negro Education* 7 (April 1938) 190–92.

———. "Journey to Accompong." Review of *Katherine Dunham's Journey to Accompong* by Katherine Dunham. *Journal of Negro Education* 16 (Spring 1947): 201–02.

———. "The Negro in the Americas." Review of *Slave and Citizen: The Negro in the Americas* by Frank Tannenbaum. *Journal of Negro Education* 16 (Spring 1947), 199–201.

———. Review of *Black Venus* by André Salmon. *Opportunity* 8 (June 1930): 185–86.

———. Review of *Classified Catalogue of Collections of Anti-Slavery Propaganda in Oberlin College Library* by F. Hubbard. *Opportunity* 11 (February 1933): 57–59.

———. Review of *County Library Service in the South: A Study of the Rosenwald County Library Demonstration* by Louis R. Wilson and Edward A. Wright. *Journal of Negro Education* 6 (January 1937): 78–81.

———. Review of *The First Negro Medical Society: A History of the Medico-Chirurgical Society of the District of Columbia, 1884–1939* by William M. Cobb. *Journal of Negro Education* 9 (April 1940): 213–15.

———. Review of *Sad-Faced Boy* by Arna Bontemps. *Negro History Bulletin* 1 (December 1937): 8.

———. Review of *The Southern Negro and the Public Library* by Eliza A. Gleason. *Social Forces* 20 (May 1942): 512–13.

Bibliography

Preface and Chapter 1

Botnick, Julie. "'I Am Sure That You Know Yourself That It Is a Very Good Job": The Early Life and Library of Dorothy Porter." Student paper. New Haven, CT: Yale University, 2014. http://www.library.yale.edu/~nkuhl/YCALStudentWork/Botnick_Porter_Paper.pdf.

Burnett, Bertha Bell. Unpublished Memoir. JWJ MSS 93, Box 111, Dorothy Porter Wesley Papers, James Weldon Johnson Collection in the Yale Collection of American Literature, Beinecke Rare Book and Manuscript Library, New Haven, CT.

Gustee Burnett to Dorothy Porter. Letter dated January 20, 1930. JWJ MSS 93, Box 35, Dorothy Porter Wesley Papers, James Weldon Johnson Collection in the Yale Collection of American Literature, Beinecke Rare Book and Manuscript Library, New Haven, CT.

Muganda, Janice. "A Brief Study of Mrs. Dorothy Burnett Porter: From Birth to Completion of High School, 1905–1922." Unpublished paper, Howard University, 1972. JWJ MSS 93, Box 111, Dorothy Porter Wesley Papers, James Weldon Johnson Collection in the Yale Collection of American Literature, Beinecke Rare Book and Manuscript Library, New Haven, CT.

Porter, Dorothy B. "Fifty Years of Collecting," In *Black Access: A Bibliography of Afro-American Bibliographies*, compiled by Richard Newman. Westport, CT: Greenwood Press, 1984.

Sandford, Ann. "Rescuing Ernestine Rose (1880–1961): Harlem Librarian and Social Activist." *Long Island History Journal* 22 (Summer 2011): 1–9. http://lihj.cc.stonybrook.edu/media/22-2/Sandford22-2.pdf.

Wikipedia. "Normal School for Colored Girls." http://en.wikipedia.org/wiki/Normal_School_for_Colored_Girls.

CHAPTER 2

Battle, Thomas C. "Moorland Spingarn Research Center." *Library Quarterly* 58 (1988): 143–63. http://www.howard.edu/msrc/about_history.html.

Dyson, Walter. *Howard University: The Capstone of Negro Education, A History: 1867–1940*. Washington, D.C.: The Graduate School Howard University, 1941.

Howard University. "Brief History of Howard University." http://www.howard.edu/explore/history.htm.

Howard University Library System. "The Founders Library." http://library.howard.edu/Founders.

"The J.E. Moorland Foundation of the University Library." *Howard University Record*, 10 (January 1916): 3–15.

Jones, Ida E. *The Heart of the Race Problem: The Life of Kelly Miller*. Littleton, MA: Tapestry Press, 2011.

Logan, Rayford W. *Howard University: The First Hundred Years, 1867–1967*. New York: New York University Press, 1969.

Logan, Rayford W., and Michael R. Winston. *Dictionary of American Negro Biography*. New York: W.W. Norton, 1982.

Madison, Avril Johnson, and Dorothy Porter Wesley. "Dorothy Burnett Porter Wesley: Enterprising Steward of Black Culture." *The Pubic Historian* 17 (Winter 1995): 15–40.

Mills, Paul T., Sr. "Edward Christopher Williams, 1871–December 24, 1929." The Black Renaissance in Washington. http://dclibrarylabs.org/blkren/bios/williamsec.html.

Porter, Dorothy B. "Fifty Years of Collecting," In *Black Access: A Bibliography of Afro-American Bibliographies*, compiled by Richard Newman. Westport, CT: Greenwood Press, 1984.

Scarupa, Harriet Jackson. "The Energy-Charged Life of Dorothy Porter Wesley." *New Directions: The Howard University Magazine* 17 (January 1990): 6–17.

Winston, Michael R. "Moorland-Spingarn Research Center: A Past Revisited, A Present Reclaimed." *New Directions: The Howard University Magazine* 1 (Summer 1974): 19–25.

CHAPTER 3

Battle, Thomas C. "Dorothy Louise Burnett Porter Wesley (1905–1995)." In *Dictionary of American Library Biography*, edited by Donald David. Westport, CT: Libraries Unlimited, 2003.

Bhan, Esme. "Legacy of a Job Well Done." *Washington Post*, December 31, 1995, E5.

Bontemps, Arna. "Special Collections of Negroana." *Library Quarterly* XIV (July 1944): 187–200.

Dorothy Porter "List of Trips." Memorandum dated 1946. JWJ MSS 93, Box 6, Dorothy Porter Wesley Papers, James Weldon Johnson Collection in the Yale Collection of American Literature, Beinecke Rare Book and Manuscript Library, New Haven, CT.

Dorothy Porter Wesley to National Arts and Humanities Foundation. Letter dated May 24, 1966. JWJ MSS 93, Box 93, Dorothy Porter Wesley Papers, James Weldon Johnson Collection in the Yale Collection of American Literature, Beinecke Rare Book and Manuscript Library, New Haven, CT.

Dyson, Walter. *Howard University: The Capstone of Negro Education, A History: 1867–1940*. Washington, D.C.: Graduate School of Howard University, 1941.

Ford Foundation. *Inclusive Scholarship: Developing Black Studies in the United States: A 25th Anniversary Retrospective of Ford Foundation Grants, 1982–2007*. Report. http://www.fordfoundation.org/pdfs/library/inclusive_scholarship.pdf.

"Howard University Acquires the Most Comprehensive Collection of Works by Negro Authors in the World." *Howard University Bulletin* 48 (December 1948): 3.

Kelly Miller to F.D. Buford. Letter dated July 18, 1938. Kelly Miller Papers, Box 71-1, Folder 18. Manuscript Division. Moorland-Spingarn Research Center, Howard University, Washington, D.C.

Kelly Miller to T.L. Hungate. Letter dated August 1, 1938. Kelly Miller Papers, Box 71-1, Folder 14. Manuscript Division. Moorland-Spingarn Research Center, Howard University, Washington, D.C.

Leffall, Dolores. "Dorothy Porter Wesley." Telephone interview with Janet Sims-Wood. June 17, 2014.

"Porter Directs Mooreland [*sic*] Room." *The Hilltop*, October 15, 1971, 8.

Porter, Dorothy B. *Moorland Foundation Annual Reports*. Washington, D.C.: Howard University, 1932–73.

Scarupa, Harriet. "The Energy-Charged Life of Dorothy Porter Wesley." *New Directions: The Howard University Magazine* 17 (January 1990): 6–17.

Trescott, Jacqueline. "Chatelaine of Black History." *Sunday Star and Daily News*, June 24, 1973, G1, G12.

Wesley, Dorothy Porter. "Black Antiquarians and Bibliophiles Revisited, with a Glance at Today's Lovers of Books and Memorabilia." In *Black Bibliophiles and Collectors: Preservers of Black History*, edited by Elinor

DesVerney Sinnette, W. Paul Coates and Thomas C. Battle. Washington, D.C.: Howard University Press, 1990.

CHAPTER 4

Battle, Thomas. "Dorothy Porter Wesley." Interview with Janet Sims-Wood. April 28, 2014.

Bracey, John. "Dorothy Porter Wesley." E-mail to Janet Sims-Wood. May 13, 2014.

Clark, John Rodney. "The Consummate Librarian." *Washington Post*, December 22, 1989.

Davis, Arthur P. "Tribute to Dorothy Porter Wesley." JWJ MSS 93, Box 101, Dorothy Porter Wesley Papers, James Weldon Johnson Collection in the Yale Collection of American Literature, Beinecke Rare Books and Manuscripts Library, New Haven, CT.

Harley, Sharon. "Dorothy Porter Wesley. "Telephone interview with Janet Sims-Wood. May 20, 2014.

Hine, Darlene Clark. "Dorothy Porter Wesley." E-mail to Janet Sims-Wood. May 13, 2014.

Josey, E.J., and Marva L. DeLoach. *Ethnic Collections in Libraries*. New York: Neal-Schuman, 1983.

Katz, William Loren. *Eyewitness: The Negro in American History*. Belmont, CA: Fearon Pitman Publishers, 1974.

Langston Hughes to Dorothy Porter. "Negro History Week Program." Letter dated February 19, 1949. JWJ MSS 93, Box 111, Dorothy Porter Wesley Papers, James Weldon Johnson Collection in the Yale Collection of American Literature, Beinecke Rare Books and Manuscripts Library, New Haven, CT.

Meier, August. *Negro Thought in America, 1880–1915*. Ann Arbor: University of Michigan Press, 1964.

Porter, Dorothy B. *Annual Report for the Moorland-Foundation*. Washington, D.C.: Howard University, 1932.

Richardson, Marilyn. "Dorothy Porter Wesley." E-mail to Janet Sims-Wood. June 20, 2014.

Sales, Ruby. "Dorothy Porter Wesley." Telephone interview with Janet Sims-Wood. June 29, 2014.

Scarupa, Harriet. "The Energy-Charged Life of Dorothy Porter Wesley." *New Directions: The Howard University Magazine* 17 (January 1990): 6–17.

Seon, Yvonne. "Dorothy Porter Wesley." E-mail to Janet Sims-Wood. June 21, 2014.

Sinnette, Elinor Des Verney. "Dorothy Porter Wesley." Telephone interview with Janet Sims-Wood. June 25, 2014.

CHAPTER 5

Battle, Thomas C. "Dorothy Porter Wesley: Preserver of Black History— Afro-American Librarian." Diverse Education (June 16, 2007). http:// diverseeducation.com/article/7457/.

"BCALA 20th Anniversary Awards: Trailblazer Award." *BCALA Newsletter* 19 (August 1990): 5.

Benjamin Quarles to Dorothy Porter. Letter dated May 11, 1972. Dorothy Porter Wesley Papers, JWJ MSS 93, Box 97, James Weldon Johnson Collection in the Yale Collection of American Literature, Beinecke Rare Book and Manuscript Library, New Haven, CT.

Bourne, Kay. "Historian's Gravesite Finally Gets Marker." *Bay State Banner*, October 5, 1989, 1, 12.

Bracey, John. "Dorothy Porter Wesley." E-mail to Janet Sims-Wood. May 13, 2014.

Burkett, Nancy, and Randall Burkett. "Obituaries—Dorothy Burnett Porter Wesley." Proceedings of the American Antiquarian Society, 1996. http:// www.americanantiquarian.org/proceedings/44539475.pdf

Burkett, Randall. "Dorothy Porter Wesley." E-mail to Janet Sims-Wood. May 19, 2014.

Coates, W. Paul. "Dorothy Porter Wesley." Telephone interview with Janet Sims-Wood. April 7, 2014.

Dawson, Alma. "Celebrating African American Librarians and Librarianship." *Library Trends* 49 (Summer 2000): 49–87.

Des Jardins, Jules. "Black Librarians and the Search for Women's Biography During the New Negro History Movement." *OAH: Magazine of History* 20 (January 2006): 15–18.

Dorothy Porter to Fred Anthoensen. Letter dated January 14, 1953. Dorothy Porter Wesley Papers, JWJ MSS 93, Box 6, James Weldon Johnson Collection in the Yale Collection of American Literature, Beinecke Rare Book and Manuscript Library, New Haven, CT.

Dorothy Porter to Langston Hughes. Letter dated April 23, 1965. Dorothy Porter Wesley Papers, JWJ MSS 93, Box 1, James Weldon Johnson Collection in the Yale Collection of American Literature, Beinecke Rare Book and Manuscript Library, New Haven, CT.

Dorothy Porter Wesley to G.K. Hall. Letter dated October 31, 1995. Dorothy Porter Wesley Papers, JWJ MSS 93, Box 1, James Weldon Johnson

Collection in the Yale Collection of American Literature, Beinecke Rare Book and Manuscript Library, New Haven, CT.

Jefferson, Karen. "Dorothy Porter Wesley: A Lifelong Commitment to the Preservation of Black History." Unpublished paper. ASALH 75th Anniversary Conference. 1990. Dorothy Porter Wesley Papers, JWJ MSS 93, Box 97, James Weldon Johnson Collection in the Yale Collection of American Literature, Beinecke Rare Book and Manuscript Library, New Haven, CT.

Langston Hughes to Dorothy Porter. Letter dated May 9, 1965. Dorothy Porter Wesley Papers, JWJ MSS 93, Box 1, James Weldon Johnson Collection in the Yale Collection of American Literature, Beinecke Rare Book and Manuscript Library, New Haven, CT.

Leffall, Dolores. "Dorothy Porter Wesley." Telephone interview with Janet Sims-Wood. June 17, 2014.

McElrath, Susan. "Bethune Museum and Archives, Inc." *Mid Atlantic Archivist-MARAC Newsletter* (Summer 1993): 20.

Porter, Dorothy B. *Annual Report for the Moorland-Foundation.* Washington, D.C.: Howard University, 1954.

———. "Bibliography and Research in Afro-American Scholarship." *Journal of Academic Librarianship* 2 (May 1976): 77, 80.

———. "Fifty Years of Collecting." In *Black Access: A Bibliography of Afro-American Bibliophiles.* Compiled by Richard Newman. Westport, CT: Greenwood Press.

Richardson, Marilyn. "Dorothy Porter Wesley." E-mail to Janet Sims-Wood. June 20, 2014.

Scarupa, Harriet. "The Energy-Charged Life of Dorothy Porter Wesley." *New Directions: The Howard University Magazine* 17 (January 1990): 6–17.

Weeks, Linton. "The Undimmed Light of Black History: Dorothy Porter, Collecting Forgotten Memories." *Washington Post,* November 15, 1995, C1.

Wesley, Dorothy Porter. "Foreword." In *Catalogue of the Charles L. Blockson Afro-American Collection: A Unit of the Temple University Libraries.* Philadelphia: Temple University Press, 1990.

"William Cooper Nell—Program." Dorothy Porter Wesley Papers, JWJ MSS 93, Box 97, James Weldon Johnson Collection in the Yale Collection of American Literature, Beinecke Rare Book and Manuscript Library, New Haven, CT.

Yale University. "Black Abolitionists Papers." http://bap.chadwyck.com/marketing/about_bap.jsp.

CHAPTER 6

Battle, Thomas. "Dorothy Porter Wesley." Telephone interview with Janet Sims-Wood. April 28, 2014.

Burkett, Nancy, and Randall Burkett. "Obituaries—Dorothy Burnett Porter Wesley." Proceeding of the American Antiquarian Society 1996. http://www.americanantiquarian.org/proceedings/44539475.pdf.

Burkett, Randall. "Dorothy Porter Wesley. E-mail to Janet Sims-Wood. May 19, 2014.

Coates to Porter. "Black Bibliophiles Symposium Thank You." Letter dated April 5, 1983. JWJ MSS 93, Box 106, Dorothy Porter Wesley Papers, James Weldon Johnson Collection in the Yale Collection of American Literature, Beinecke Rare Book and Manuscript Library, New Haven, CT.

Coates, W. Paul. "Dorothy Porter Wesley." Telephone interview with Janet Sims-Wood. April 7, 2014.

Davis, Arthur P. "Introduction of Dorothy Porter at the 1973 Charles Eaton Burch Lecture." JWJ MSS 93, Box 97, Dorothy Porter Wesley Papers, James Weldon Johnson Collection in the Yale Collection of American Literature, Beinecke Rare Book and Manuscript Library, New Haven, CT.

"Du Bois Institute Celebrates Endowed Fund for Research." *Harvard University Gazette*, June 3, 1994, 1, 6.

McCombs, Phil. "Touching History at Howard; University's Library of Black Culture Celebrates 75 Years of Growth." *Washington Post*, December 16, 1989, D1.

Michael R. Winston to Dorothy Porter Wesley. Letter dated June 2, 1977. JWJ MSS 93, Box 102, Dorothy Porter Wesley Papers, James Weldon Johnson Collection in the Yale Collection of American Literature, Beinecke Rare Book and Manuscript Library, New Haven, CT.

———. Letter dated February 12, 1979. JWJ MSS 93, Box 102, Dorothy Porter Wesley Papers, James Weldon Johnson Collection in the Yale Collection of American Literature, Beinecke Rare Book and Manuscript Library, New Haven, CT.

Porter, Dorothy. "Bibliography and Research in Afro-American Scholarship." *Journal of Academic Librarianship* 2 (May 1976): 81.

———. "Memorandum to Joseph Reason—Trips Made to Philadelphia and New York." Memorandum dated November 1946. JWJ MSS 93, Box 6, Dorothy Porter Wesley Papers, James Weldon Johnson Collection in the Yale Collection of American Literature, Beinecke Rare Book and Manuscript Library, New Haven, CT.

———. "Once a Librarian, Always a Librarian." JWJ MSS 93, Box 97, Dorothy Porter Wesley Papers, James Weldon Johnson Collection in the Yale Collection of American Literature, Beinecke Rare Book and Manuscript-Library, New Haven, CT.

Pyne, Charlynn Spencer. "A Wealth of African American Resources: Scholars' Use of LC Collections Inspires Seminar." *Library of Congress Information Bulletin*, April 18, 1994. http://loc.gov/loc/lcib/94/9408/seminar.html.

Recent Notable Books: A Selected Bibliography in Honor of Dorothy Porter Wesley. Washington, D.C.: Moorland-Spingarn Research Center, 1974.

Scarupa, Harriet. "The Energy-Charged Life of Dorothy Porter Wesley." *New Directions: The Howard University Magazine* 17 (January 1990): 6–17.

Wesley, Dorothy Porter. "Black Antiquarians and Bibliophiles Revisited, with a Glance at Today's Lovers of Books and Memorabilia." In *Black Bibliophiles and Collectors: Preservers of Black History*, edited by Elinor Des Verney Sinnette, W. Paul Coates and Thomas C. Battle. Washington, D.C.: Howard University Press, 1990.

CHAPTER 7

Beinecke Staff. "Guide to the Dorothy Porter Wesley Papers." JWJ MSS 93. March 2013. Beinecke Rare Book and Manuscript Library, Yale University, New Haven, CT.

Botnick, Julie. "'I Am Sure That You Know Yourself That It Is a Very Good Job": The Early Life and Library of Dorothy Porter." Student paper. New Haven, CT: Yale University, 2014. http://www.library.yale.edu/~nkuhl/YCALStudentWork/Botnick_Porter_Paper.pdf (accessed May 31, 2014).

Burch, Audra D.S. "Treasure Trove of Black History: Lauderdale Woman Seeks Home for Collection." *Miami Herald*, August 25, 1999, 1, 4.

Constance Porter Wesley to Samuel F. Morrison. Unsigned letter draft dated August 30, 1999. JWJ MSS 93 Box 101, Dorothy Porter Wesley Papers, James Weldon Johnson Collection in the Yale Collection of American Literature, Beinecke Rare Book and Manuscript Library, New Haven, CT.

Jane S. Knowles to Constance Porter Uzelac. Letter dated July 11, 2000. JWJ MSS 93 Box 102, Dorothy Porter Wesley Papers, James Weldon Johnson Collection in the Yale Collection of American Literature, Beinecke Rare Book and Manuscript Library, New Haven, CT.

———. Letter dated December 11, 2000. JWJ MSS 93 Box 102, Dorothy Porter Wesley Papers, James Weldon Johnson Collection in the Yale Collection of American Literature, Beinecke Rare Book and Manuscript Library, New Haven, CT.

Luzia, Kala A. "Dorothy Porter Wesley Collection, 1852–1995." Broward County Library African American Research Library and Cultural Center. http://caad.library.miami.edu/?p=collections/findingaid&id=21&disab letheme=1.

The Root. "Obituary of Constance Porter Uzelac." http://announcements. theroot.com/announcements/obituary-of-constance-porter-uzelac.

Sun Sentinel. "Coni Porter Uzelac Obituary." May 2, 2012. http:// www.legacy.com/obituaries/sunsentinel/obituary.aspx?n=coni-uzelac&pid=157395973.

Swann Auction Galleries. "Printed and Manuscript African Americana." February 25, 2010, Sale 2204, Lot 141 [James Amos Porter, 15 large cartons]. http://catalogue.swanngalleries.com/asp/fullCatalogue.asp?sa lelot=2204+++++141+&refno=++627661&saletype=.

———. "Printed and Manuscript African Americana." March 10, 2011, Sale 2239, Lot 281 [Charles Harris Wesley, 35 cartons]. http://catalogue. swanngalleries.com/asp/fullCatalogue.asp?salelot=2239+++++281+& refno=++642624&saletype=.

———. "Printed and Manuscript African Americana." March 1, 2012, Sale 2271, Lot 296 [Dorothy Porter Wesley, 85 cartons]. "http://catalogue. swanngalleries.com/asp/fullCatalogue.asp?salelot=2271+++++296+& refno=++655495&saletype=.

University of Miami Libraries Collaborative Archive from the African Diaspora. "Dorothy Porter Wesley Collection, 1852–1995." http://caad. library.miami.edu/?p=collections/controlcard&id=21.

Wesley, Dorothy Porter. "Black Antiquarians and Bibliophiles Revisited, with a Glance at Today's Lovers of Books and Memorabilia." In *Black Bibliophiles and Collectors: Preservers of Black History*, edited by Elinor Des Verney Sinnette, W. Paul Coates and Thomas C. Battle. Washington, D.C.: Howard University Press, 1990.

APPENDIXES

Britton, Helen H. "Dorothy Porter Wesley: A Bibliographic Profile." In *American Black Women in the Arts and Social Sciences: A Bibliographical Survey*, by Ora Williams. Metchuen, NJ: Scarecrow, 1994, 20–23.

———. "Dorothy Porter Wesley: A Bibliographer, Curator, and Scholar." In *Reclaiming the American Library Past: Writing in the Women*, edited by Suzanne Hildenbrand. Norwood, NJ: Ablex Publishing Corporation, 1996. 163–86.

Moses, Sibyl E. *African American Women Writers in New Jersey, 1836–2000: A Biographical Dictionary and Bibliographic Guide.* New Brunswick, NJ: Rutgers University Press, 2003. 198–207.

INDEX

T

Tappan, Lewis 31, 35

U

Uzelac, Constance Porter 16, 86, 108, 115, 116, 117, 119

W

W.E.B. Du Bois Institute for African and African American Research 70, 85, 86, 101, 102, 103

Wesley, Charles H. 15, 42, 63, 71, 73, 85, 95, 115

Williams, Edward Christopher 35, 36, 38

Winston, Michael R. 62, 91, 95, 98, 105, 108, 110

Women's Studies 69, 71, 72, 80, 81

Woodson, Carter G. 75, 89

Y

Yale University 15, 16, 19

Yale University Beinecke Rare Book and Manuscript Library 19, 119, 120

ABOUT THE AUTHOR

Dr. Janet Sims-Wood retired as assistant chief librarian of the Moorland-Spingarn Research Center, Howard University. She currently serves as an associate professor/adjunct faculty librarian at Prince George's Community College (PGCC) in Largo, Maryland. She was a founding associate editor of *SAGE: A Scholarly Journal on Black Women* (1984–94). She is a member of the Maryland Humanities Council Speakers Bureau and currently serves as national vice-president of the Association for the Study of African American Life and History (ASALH). She is a commissioner on the Maryland Commission on African American History and Culture. In 2013, Dr. Sims-Wood received a Created Equal: America's Civil Rights Struggle grant from the National Endowment for the Humanities, and in 2014 she received a PGCC Pathfinder grant for travel to Yale University to conduct research in the Dorothy Porter Wesley Papers. She also received the 2014 James Partridge Outstanding Award for African American Information Professionals presented by the University of Maryland College of Information Studies and Citizens for Maryland Libraries. She is a life member of ASALH and the Association of Black Women Historians (ABWH).

Lonnie Dawkins Photography.

CPSIA information can be obtained
at www.ICGtesting.com
Printed in the USA
LVHW080621160322
713572LV00005B/395